A STATEMENT BY
ADMIRAL WILLIAM F. HALSEY

Aircraft Carrier is intensely interesting and is fascinating reading. I have spent over four years in carriers, as Commanding Officer and as a Flag Officer. These included the original *Saratoga, Lexington* and the still extant and justly famous *Enterprise*. The first six months of World War II I had my flag on the *Enterprise*.

How vividly this remarkable book by Joe Bryan, my good friend, brought before me things blurred and half forgotten, due to the passage of time. His descriptions excellently portray events that were of almost daily occurrence.

While in command of the Third Fleet, I had many carriers serving under me and I was in close touch with them for days on end. I saw them hit with Kamikaze planes, I saw them burn. I saw the clouds of smoke and flames ascending high in the air above their decks. I saw them keep going, finally controlling the fires and damage, and these magnificent ships brought into port. They were repaired and returned to fight again.

This yarn in diary form contains an almost blow by blow account of the youngsters, the magnificent youngsters, who flew and fought our planes from the Fleet. Joe Bryan gives you an insight into their daily lives, their thoughts, their superstitions, their reactions. When reading remember that almost daily they faced death. *Aircraft Carrier* portrays how they met this threat. It gives a vivid picture of the United States secret weapon, the youth of America. What a debt of gratitude we owe them! It equally portrays the shipboard men who faced the Kamikaze threat, and all phases of shipboard life under war conditions.

The intimate glimpses of the daily lives of these men show they were neither saints nor sinners, just good average American boys, who were tried and found not wanting under the acid test of war. They had mental, moral and, yes, spiritual qualities of high order. When evening prayers were held daily through the ship's loud-speakers it was an inspiring sight to see the reverent attitude of men throughout the ship.

At times it was my misfortune to have to force these men almost to the point of exhaustion. They showed the stuff they were made of. Of course, being good sailormen they groused a bit, but always bounced back. They realized that although they were near the breaking point, the Japs were being pushed beyond the breaking point, and they kept pouring on the pressure. As an old Navy man I am proud of each and every one of them.

This is one of the best stories of the human side of shipboard life during war conditions that has been published. Every good American should read it. To the wartime sailor it will bring back vividly many memories. To those who know little about shipboard life, it will afford a chance to renew their faith and pride in the U. S. Navy.

AIRCRAFT CARRIER

by

J. BRYAN, III
Lieutenant Commander, USNR

BALLANTINE BOOKS • NEW YORK

PRINTING HISTORY

FIRST PRINTING: FEBRUARY, 1954
Published March, 1954
SECOND PRINTING: AUGUST, 1957

BALLANTINE BOOKS, INC.
101 Fifth Avenue, New York 3, N. Y.

FOREWORD

This book is a reproach to my fairly recent male ancestors. It's also to keep my descendants from reproaching me.

My father was a captain in the Air Corps in World War I, but he never wrote a word about what he saw. Neither did Grandfather, a nineteen-year-old trooper in Company D, 43rd Battalion, Virginia Cavalry—Mosby's Raiders. He was wounded twice in his first ten days in uniform, and Captain Mountjoy called him "one of the old blue hen's chickens," but I have no idea whether he wore a saber, or what his horse's name was, or how he felt during the ambush at Berry's Ferry.

Grandfather's elder brother, Randolph, was just twenty in the spring of '62, when General Johnston borrowed him and sent him up in a balloon, to map McClellan's dispositions around Yorktown. Uncle Ran had never even seen a balloon before; this one was made of tarred cotton, lifted by hot air from a pine-knot fire. It bounced and rocked and whirled him sick and dizzy, but he drew his maps and gave them to Johnston, then asked him, "Will you not now, sir, reassign me to my former place with General Magruder?"

Johnston's smile was lined with sharp teeth. "Sir," he said, "you forget that you are my only experienced aeronaut. Pray hold yourself in readiness for another ascension at any time."

It was Johnston who told the story, not Uncle Ran. . . .

I often thought of Uncle Ran, when I was flying in the Pacific. I wondered if he, too, carried a luckpiece, and if he, too, eventually learned not to eat onions before an "ascension." I wished he had kept a diary or at least left some notes, but he didn't.

To be sure, Great-Grandfather kept a diary of sorts, when he was a midshipman on the *United States*. I have a copy. Entry after entry says only, "Day commenced with a calm; about 5 P.M. a light breeze sprung up," or, "This morning we carried away our main topgallant yard." He never gives any details, even when you'd think they would have forced themselves onto the page, as here, "June 13, 1824. Reported 8 o'clock to Captain Carter, lying on the cabin floor unable to rise." *Why* unable? Sick? Drunk? Presumably the latter, because an entry three months later says, "Charges have been preferred against Captain Carter by one of his officers."

I wish you had told us a little more, sir, and it is inexcusable of you to omit—not skimp, but *omit*—your duel with Midshipman Doyle. If your mother's uncle hadn't chanced by and written her about it, we might never have known that you "shot off the butt of the adversary's pistol and severely wounded his right hand." Congratulations, sir! (And thanks for not getting killed.)

Well, reading the scanty records of these old young warriors, and watching their legends blur, I resolved that if ever I went to war, I'd try to distill and bottle some of my ferment. Orginally, my sole hope was to slake the Nth generation's curiosity about a certain link in the long chain from Adam to themselves. But as practice sharpened my eyes and ears, I found that I was also eager to preserve as much as possible of the incomparable wit and courage of my shipmates—fragments precious to naval historians, but irretrievable save from collections by "such maggotieheaded fellowes as myself," in John Aubrey's phrase.

I am aware, of course, of the official regulation against naval diaries. In 1945, though, when I was ordered to the *Yorktown,* I was given special permission for a diary. In fact, I was instructed to keep one, for a reason no longer of interest. Here is the result, exactly as I first wrote it, except for deletions of a few technical passages and of a few others which now strike me as perhaps too intimate. For any reader who likes to picture the writer, I was forty years old at the time, and a lieutenant commander in the Naval Reserve. The reader may also enjoy being reminded that Admiral Radford is now Chairman of the Joint Chiefs of Staff and that Jimmy Smith is now Assistant Secretary of the Navy for Air.

J. BRYAN, III

January 30, 1945. Pearl Harbor

George Bond said, "Nonsense! *You* on a carrier? Why, they must have—— Let's see those orders of yours."

I handed them over.

He mumbled a few lines, then stabbed the paper with his finger. "Just as I thought! They left out a word. See where it reads 'Carrier Division Six'? What they *meant* to write was 'Carrier *Pigeon* Division Six.' That's it. They'll start you on cleaning the coops, and after a few months, if you show any aptitude, they may promote you to giving the pigeons a rub-down when they come back from their hops. Now, when I was ACIO on the *Monterey*——"

John McClain said, "CARDIV Six? Who's your admiral?"

"Rear Admiral Radford."

"What's his flagship?"

"Ticonderoga."

We were sitting in his office at the Fleet Motion Picture headquarters in Honolulu. McClain said, "Wait a minute. We've got a film of her around here somewhere—taken off Formosa last week and came in yesterday. Go into the projection room, and I'll have it run for you."

It was a very short film. It simply showed two Jap planes plunging through the *Ticonderoga's* flight deck, two tremendous explosions, and smoke and flames pouring out of the ship. The next film showed a Jap plane plunging through the *Intrepid's* flight deck. The third film showed a third carrier. . . .

The lights went up. McClain said, "You're going to have a million laughs out there, chum—a million of 'em! Those crazy Japs can't fly for nuts. Notice how they get right over a ship, and then just lose control of the plane, and fall right on top of you? Ever see anything as ridiculous in your life? Hell, it's better than a Benchley short! You'll be rolling on the deck all day long!"

February 4th (Sunday). Ulithi

(Ulithi atoll, which lies about 400 miles southwest of Guam, had been occupied without opposition on 23 September 1944, as part of the Western Carolines operation. The atoll encloses a harbor capable of sheltering 1,000 ships, and its principal islands—Asor, Mog Mog, and Falalap—provided room for shore installations, an airstrip, and a recreation area.)

I flew from Pearl to Guam, and from Guam down here. A small boat took me out to the *Ticonderoga*. A fortnight had passed since the two *kamikazes* had hit her, but she was still a sick ship, smelling of death and ashes. Rain dripped through the holes in her flight deck and trickled down the bulkheads, making sooty streaks. Fragments of the Jap planes had been collected and laid out on the hanger deck. Almost every scrap bore a label, with the name of the man who had picked it up and a request that it be returned to him as a souvenir, when the Tech Intelligence officers had finished their examination.

Sherbie Becker, the *Ti's* Air Combat Intelligence officer, told me that when the attack came he'd happened to be out of his office, and when he went back to it a jagged piece of steel eight inches long and smoking hot, was lying in his chair. A pilot, he said, had left two bottles of gin in the safe above his desk. Although the fires hadn't actually reached that room, both bottles had blown their corks and boiled half away. The crew was haggard and jumpy. Officers and men killed or missing, 140; wounded, more than 200.

Sherbie also told me that Admiral Radford and his staff were not aboard; they were off looking for another flagship. I had nothing to do until they returned, so I dumped my gear in Sherbie's room and set out on a "refresher" tour of the ship. As I passed near the quarter-deck, a gong rang, a pipe shrilled, and the squawk-box announced, "Admiral, U.S. Navy!" Over the side came Admiral Halsey, in shorts. As he stepped aboard, a sour voice muttered, "Jesus Christ! Sixteen spindle-legged ensigns will come out in them goddam things tomorrow!"

It was the chief master-at-arms, a grizzled, seamy old shellback who had probably been doing his third hitch when the Admiral was a naval cadet. Before he rolled away in disgust, I saw that H, O, L, D was tattooed across his left knuckles, and F, A, S, T across his right.

February 5th. Ulithi

Word comes that the *Ti* will have to go home for repairs, and Admiral Radford's flag will shift to the *Yorktown*, a few berths away. I haven't been aboard her for nine months, and then only as a short-ride passenger—Pearl to Majuro, in the Marshalls—but I remember her as a smart ship with the second-best chow I've had in the Navy. (The *Massachusetts* served the best and the *Lexington* the worst; Isaiah might have had the *Lex* in mind when he wrote, "Broth of abominable things is in their vessels.") The *Yorktown* was not only smart but—more important—she was happy. Most important of all, she was lucky.

Some ships seem to be jinxed almost from the day they're launched—the *Intrepid,* for instance, which has spent so much time in drydock that she's known throughout the fleet as the "Decrepit" and the "Dry I." Maybe their christening champagne was flat, or their sponsors didn't meet Poseidon's classic standards. I don't know. But I do know that there *are* such ships, just as others are his special pets. He soothes the storms around them, alerts them when the enemy is sneaking in, and protects them from *kamikazes,* shells, bombs, torpedoes and all such "things that go bump in the night." The *Yorktown,* the "Fighting Lady," has a reputation as one of these pets. Understatement: I hope she stays so.

I hitched a ride across to the *Yorktown,* reported to the Chief of Staff, Capt. Fred Trapnell, paid my respects to the Admiral, and checked in at the flag office. Second piece of luck: the Flag Secretary is Wellington Henderson, whom I'd hardly seen since college. He took me down to my room. There was a moment before I realized why it looked familiar: it was Number 255, the same room I'd had on the *Lexington.* This is more luck. Since the *Yorktown* is a sister-ship of the *Lex,* it means that the first time general quarters rings in the dead of the night, I won't have to fumble along a lot of strange, blacked-out passageways and ladders to find my way topside; I can get there in my sleep. Even the spacing of the second-deck coamings is the same: from my door to the foot of the hangar-deck ladder, they come at six steps, then four steps, then six, then four. I've got scars that show

how long it took me to learn the *Lex's* layout and I don't think my shins would survive indoctrination in a new one.

Hendy told me that Jimmy Smith, another old friend, was on the staff as assistant Air Operations Officer. Just then my roommate came in—Stewart Lindsay, one of the staff Communications officers—and in no time we discovered we had more mutual friends than two jailhouse cats. When I think of other ships and staffs where I've reported without knowing a soul, and that dreary period when you droop around like a kid who enters school in the middle of the term——!

But there's still that first meal in the wardroom, and the "feeling out" when you and your tablemates push words until you find something in common. I needn't have worried. A few seats away is Cooper Bright, balder and noisier than ever, and with a bigger grin; he's the ship's Air Operations officer, as he was when I was a passenger. Across from Coop is Joe Moody, the Catholic chaplain, a former shipmate on the *Massachusetts,* and one of the finest in the whole fleet. And there, jumping up from the next table, is Harwell Proffitt, whom I haven't seen since we were both on the staff of COMAIRSOWESPAC, in Australia two years ago.

Proff was a Communications watch officer then, known as "the Tattered Ensign." Now he's a lieutenant, a ship's officer, studying navigation. Nearly three years of foreign duty haven't changed his Tennessee accent at all: "You old stinker, did you know Ah got me a brahd? Yessirree. Ah'm an ole ma'ied man. They give me fo'days of honeymoon, and send me raht back to sea again. Hey, guess who's our skipper: Cap'n Combs!"

Capt. Thomas S. Combs was COMAIRSOWESPAC's Chief of Staff, and if there is a better or more popular officer in the whole United States Navy I have yet to see him. It isn't enough for me to draw a lucky, friendly ship like the *Yorktown;* "Theda" Combs turns out to be her skipper. Jackpot! (His nickname traces back to his youngster cruise, on the *Arizona.* One of his shipmates, seeing him on the way to the shower, wrapped in nothing but a towel, yelled, "There goes Theda Bara than ever!", and he's been "Theda" Combs ever since.)

Our room is on the starboard side of the second deck— the deck below the hangar deck—approximately amidships. It is about fifteen feet square and eight feet high. The room itself, and every fixture in it, is steel, painted white or gray. Beams and pipes line the outboard bulkhead, which is the side of the ship, and the overhead is a tangle of fifteen electric cables and nine more pipes. A fireproof curtain serves as a door. There is no porthole; the only light is electric, and the only ventilation comes from a blower.

Stew Lindsay and I each have a locker for our clothes, a desk and a chair, a bookshelf, and a small safe, all of them steel. We share a basin, a cabinet for toilet articles, and a fan. Nothing else is in the room. It may sound austere, but it is actually quite comfortable. The mattresses are excellent, the beds have reading lights, and the chairs are cushioned. In fact, we can file only two objections: when we turn on the water, the pipes hammer like a riveting gun; and the heat, the heat, the heat!

The whole ship is hot in this latitude (10N). The steel decks and sides soak up the sun all day and radiate it all night. My shirt is wet and sour five minutes after I've put it on. A rash has already broken out on my arms and back and under the strap of my wrist watch. My appetite is gone. I'm like an old dishrag. Salt tablets may bring relief, but I hate to swallow them; they make me sick for twenty minutes afterwards. Perhaps I ought to dissolve them in a glass of water, instead of washing them down whole. (Later: Dissolving them is the answer.)

February 6th. Ulithi

This morning our hangar deck looks like a country store after a tornado. We're loading supplies; and crates, tools, strips of metals, and cardboard cartons litter the whole forward half. Off in one corner, stacked like cordwood, are our 5-inch rockets. This is the first time I've seen them, and I'm surprised at the innocence of their appearance, which is more like a big silver pencil than anything else. I know they're murderous, but they don't look it. Nor does a bomb—just a lump of dead metal. A shell is somewhat more graceful, but it is still dead. A torpedo, though, is sleek, shining, and alive. It gives the impression of having a remorseless brain of its own—as, of course, some torpedoes really have.

Scraps: Stew Lindsay tells me the *Washington* and the *North Carolina* will be in our task group on the coming operation. I like that news. I've got a feeling we're going to need every gun we can beg or borrow.

On the flight deck, painters are outlining false elevators

11

in red. Even if the *kamikazes* are deceived into hitting them, I don't know how much we'll save by it.

An electrician's mate was working over the side in a bos'n's chair when there was a flash, and he was knocked into the water. His body did not come up.

This afternoon the ship's commanders and lieutenant commanders gave a party ashore at Mog Mog for the commanders and lieutenant commanders of the staff. Bill Ogdon and I were the only ones able to accept; the others were too busy settling in after their shift from the *Ti*. Bill used to be one of the editors of the *New York Times'* "Topic of the Times" column. Now he's the Admiral's Public Relations officer—a pipe-smoker, quiet and serious, with a face that can best be described as "medieval." The embroiderers of the Bayeux tapestry might have used him as a model.

There are a lot of big men on the *Yorktown*, but the gunnery department has the two biggest: the gun boss, George Earnshaw, the former big league pitcher, and his assistant, Pat Patterson. Almost every ship in the Navy has its professional Texan—a slow-speaking, Yankee-baiting, tall-tale-teller. Pat seems to be ours. Over the beer, we got to chatting about the old days in Espiritu Santo, and Pat asked if I remembered the possum grass there.

"Possum grass? I may have seen it, but I don't know it by that name."

"Well, you know what I mean. It's this thick green grass, acres of it, an' when you stand to winnard, it jus' lays right down an' turns brown, like it's daid. See what happens? Some cattle come by, an the grass makes out like it's daid, an' the cattle keep right on a-goin' without stoppin' to eat it, an' soon as they's gone, the ole grass turns green an' stands right up again. Don't work if you come from looard, though. I never see such a thing in my born days."

Me either. *Splendaciously mendacious rolled the Brassbound Man ashore.* . . .

Back at the ship, I was looking over the new roster of ship's and staff officers when Proff phoned me: "I see you're listed as 'Press.' If I brought a pair of pants to your room, could you get them back to me by morning?"

12

All the pilots and crewmen in our air group, AG 3, were called to the wardroom this morning for a lecture on survival, by a Marine captain. He didn't say so flatly, but his implication was unmistakable: our next target is Tokyo. As soon as it became evident, there was a flurry of whispers and nudges, then the men's faces sobered down. When they left the wardroom, they didn't laugh and jostle, as they usually do.

Fighting 3's Air Combat Intelligence officer, Ernie Stewart, told me an extraordinary incident from the recent China Sea operation. During the strike on Saigon, the fuse of a Jap AA shell hit one of the fighter pilots, Bob Thienes, in the back of his skull, punctured it, and stuck. Thienes (pronounced *Tee*-nis) was almost blinded and was only intermittently conscious, but with coaching and encouragement from his wingman, he flew 200 miles back to the ship and landed aboard safely.

It sounded like a hell of a story, so I got hold of the wingman, Bill McLeroy, and asked for details. It *is* a hell of a story! As McLeroy says, Thienes "had it as rough as a cob on a cold morning." He's now convalescing on the *Solace*, near by. If he'll talk as freely as Mac, and if I can get it down on paper——

This afternoon the staff gave a party at Asor, a little island not far from Mog Mog. We had beer and hamburgers again, with part of the ship's band playing for us, in a big open shed. Over it hung a sign with this legend: "The Shady Acres Rifle & Gun Club" and, in smaller letters, "Where Life Is a 155-mm Bore."

The guest of honor was Ernie Pyle, a bald little leprechaun who smiled seldom and said nothing, until an accordion player turned up, and from then on Pyle never left his side. The only tune he wanted to hear was "Lili Marlene." He sang it over and over again, in a thin voice, deaf to the uproar around him.

The night was clear, but ink-black, and when we headed back to the *Yorktown* we had trouble distinguishing her from the other *Essexes* around her. The *Enterprise* is unique. So is the *Saratoga*. It's impossible to mistake them. But almost the only external difference between the *Essexes* is the pattern

13

of their camouflage and such minor details as the location of their 40-mm quads. I don't believe even their skippers could tell them apart on a night like this, yet I can't imagine John Paul Jones or Captain Horatio Hornblower not being able to pick out his ship from the combined fleets of the world.

February 8th. Ulithi

The body of the man who was electrocuted day before yesterday bobbed up this morning at the exact spot where he had gone in. Nobody can explain it. The current that runs through this harbor is terrific.

Another session with McLeroy, checking the Thienes story. Afterwards, Mac and Ernie Stewart and I went out on the flight deck for a look at Air Group 3's scoreboard, on a smooth section of the island structure just below the signal bridge. Every time the air group sinks a Jap ship, a miniature ship is stenciled on the board, and every time they shoot down a Jap plane, a miniature Rising Sun flag goes up.

We were totting the score when Joe Mayer joined us. Joe is another fighter pilot, Mac's roommate, big, blond, and crop-headed. They say he'll eat anything, drink anything, fly anything, or fight anything, and no questions asked.

He glanced at the little flags and ships: "When this operation is over, there'll be a lot more of 'em up there on the island." He thought a moment, then added, "If we *have* an island. Me, I take a dim view of those *kamikazes,* dim in spades."

So does everyone else on the ship.

As we started below to the fighters' ready room, Joe pointed toward the horizon. "Here comes the *Sara,*" he said. She was hull down, but there was no mistaking her tremendous superstructure.

Joe said, "Looks like the bank building in a small town, doesn't she?"

The ready room was crowded; every seat was taken. "Never mind," McLeroy said. "Plenty of seats after this operation. We'll have some drinkin' whisky too."

"How's that?"

"We're bound to lose a lot of pilots, and when a man's shot down, we always raffle off any liquor he leaves, and I always win the raffle. I've won three so far. I'm just a lucky son of a bitch."

Joe said, "In spades. This bastard could fall into a cesspool and come up with the Russian crown jewels. Don't ever gamble with him. He'll win your hat, ass, and overcoat!"

Half an hour later, Mac had taken six dollars out of me at gin rummy. "Didn't even have any competition," he told Joe. "It was like stealin' peanuts from a gopher hole." When Mac goes gin, his shout of triumph is "Hot damn, old lady Mitchell!" These Texans!

Tonight we had the fleet premier of the *Yorktown's* personal movie, "The Fighting Lady." Half the brass hats in the Fifth Fleet came aboard to see it. The Officer of the Deck and the Junior O.O.D. nearly went crazy, ringing the right number of gongs for each of the admirals and captains, and piping them over the side. The only celebrity the crew wanted to see was Ernie Pyle. They hung on the lifelines while he climbed the gangway and they followed him almost into Admiral Radford's cabin.

Our hangar deck had been cleaned and polished until it looked like less a movie theater than an operating theater. Behind the big screen were strung signal flags spelling "YORKTOWN." The bakeshop joined the celebration with a model of the *Yorktown* afloat on a sea of pink and white icing. When Captain Combs accepted the film from Lt. Comdr. Dwight Long, who had supervised the production, he said, "We've got everything at this premiere except wet concrete for our footprints."

It's a good picture, the first I've seen that conveys any idea of the strain of carrier duty. My only regret is that there are no *kamikaze* sequences, but of course the "Divine Winds" hadn't begun to blow when "The Fighting Lady" was filmed.

In one of the flight deck scenes, I caught a flash of Al Wright in his SBD, then about three seconds' worth of Cooper Bright in air plot. Later, over coffee in the wardroom, the boys flocked around Coop, wringing his hand and begging for his autograph.

"You were marvelous!" they told him. "Never saw such a performance in my life! One minute you had me crying, the next minute I was rolling in the aisle. And that scene where she brings in the baby and shows you the resemblance, how it's bald, just like you—kid, you knocked me out of my seat! Tell us, Mr. Bright: is Marjorie Main as beautiful off the screen as she is on?"

This is probably the last movie we'll have for some time.

Scuttlebutt says we're shoving off day after tomorrow, and there's support for the Tokyo rumor in tomorrow's Plan of the Day, which was distributed late tonight: "Officers having exposed General Quarters stations will be issued special winter clothing at Compartment A-305-1AE between 0800 and 1100 today. A. S. BORN, Commander, USN, Executive Officer."

The Divine Winds may blow, but so will good winds, at least for us raw and itching victims of the heat.

February 9th. Ulithi

The emblems on all the *Yorktown's* planes are being changed today. They used to have a thin white diagonal stripe on their rudders and wing tips. Now they've got white wedges.

Originally, every Navy plane bore the type and number of its squadron in addition to its own number. For instance, you might see an Avenger marked "38 VT 29." This system was abandoned for two reasons: it gave the enemy information on the whereabouts of different squadrons, and so much white paint lessened the effectiveness of the camouflage. For a while after that, the planes bore only their own numbers, until the pilots began finding themselves joined up on another squadron, after a melée. The present system is the best. It identifies the parent carrier of the air group, without revealing it to the enemy. The *Yorktown's* identification is this white wedge. Another carrier has a diamond; a third, a checkerboard; and so on.

I drew my battle gear and checked it over in preparation for sailing tomorrow:

A helmet, painted gray. OK, after I've printed my name across it, so that somebody else won't grab it in the excitement.

A gas mask. OK, I suppose.

A rubber life belt. These are strictly no good for a topside battle station like mine. (The Chief of Staff has assigned me to flag bridge, but hasn't given me any specific battle duties as yet.) If you have to jump over the side, this sort of belt will almost certainly be torn off; and if the jump knocks your wind out, you can't blow it up. The hell with it! I turned it in for a kapok jacket, which has the additional advantage of offering some protection against splinters.

Flashproof clothing: a cotton hood, a pair of elbow-length

16

cotton gloves, a plastic eye shield, and a woolly mask for your nose and mouth. OK, if the hood, eye shield, and mask wouldn't slide over your face every time you put your helmet on, but maybe that can be fixed by sewing them together.

A waterproof flashlight, to pin on your life jacket, and a policeman's whistle on a lanyard around your neck. OK. (These are in case you go overboard in the dark.)

A windbreaker and a muffler. OK. Bridges get cold at night.

First-aid kit and a sheath knife. OK.

Binoculars and sunglasses. OK.

And that's the lot.

This afternoon I filled in the Thienes story with statements from the minor actors—the Landing Signals officer, Air Group 3's Flight Surgeon, and Gentry, the plane captain—and tonight McLeroy and I hooked a wet ride over to the *Solace* to see Thienes himself. A dark, slender boy, soft-voiced and devout, he answered my questions without the least self-consciousness, as if he himself deserved no credit for his miraculous return. His attitude was, "I planted, McLeroy watered, but God gave the increase."

I said, "I can understand how Mac guided you back to the ship, but he certainly couldn't guide you onto the flight deck, and yet you say you have no recollection of making the landing.

He smiled faintly. "Well, my wife has prayed for me every day since we sailed."

It was as simple as that.

Mac and I got home around midnight. The Plan of the Day was lying on my desk. Its last line tipped the plot: "0830. Underway for Indian Country."

February 10th. At sea

This morning, an hour before we were due to shove off, I brought my battle gear up to flag plot and stowed it under a desk where it would be handy. The TBS (radio-telephone) was already croaking away:

"Hello, Rebel Base! This is Rebel 22. Please say again your last transmission. Over!"

"Hello, Russia! This is Evergreen. How do you receive me? Over!"

"Russia" is Admiral Radford's call sign, as Commander

of Task Group 58.4. Commander Jackson, the flag Operations officer, picked up the transmitter and answered, "Hello, Evergreen! This is Russia. I receive you five by five. Out!"

Just then Captain Combs came in, chewing a cigar butt: "I knew we'd get fouled up, Admiral—all these damn DDs crowding around us! There's one right under our nose now! I've been kicking him in the pants since seven-thirty, so he'll get out in time."

He stumped up the ladder to the navigating bridge, muttering "Damn little cans!"

I went out to flag bridge. From its forward end, I could see perhaps 300° of the horizon, and in that sector I counted 184 ships of destroyer size or larger. Lord knows how many others, far away, were screened by big ships close aboard; and the southern anchorage, just as jammed as ours, was out of sight completely. This is the largest fleet I've ever seen—far larger than what we had at Majuro last year, for the Marianas operation. They're all here: battleships, battle cruisers, heavy and light crusiers, dozens of carriers, scores of destroyers, hundreds of auxiliaries——

> Like leviathans afloat,
> Lay their bulwarks in the brine.

The combat ships are "on the mark." They look taut, cocked. *Our navy is address'd, our power collected.*

The first destroyer moves out, then another, and another. The *Essex,* on our starboard beam, seems to be sliding backward. No, it's the *Yorktown* that is moving. Somehow, I had expected her to start with a jerk, like a railroad train. Next to the *Essex* is a heavy cruiser, the *Salt Lake City,* striped and checkered like a Comanche in his war paint ("under way for Indian country"). The *Sara* and the *Bunker Hill,* to port, are dark gray; so is the *Randolph.* They're not camouflaged like us and the *Bennington.*

Now the destroyers have formed a column to lead us through the torpedo net. Evidently they're slow about it, because the skipper's voice roars down from the navigating bridge, "These damn cans are indicating only nine knots! Who the hell do they belong to?"

The Admiral calls up to him, "Go ahead! They've got to get out of your way!"

"Ahead standard!" the skipper shouts, and a yellow speed cone runs up each of our outboard signal halyards.

We gather speed, slipping past the new *Alaska,* with her

horned stack. Still the destroyers linger almost under our bows. The Admiral begins to fume: "Goddam it, doesn't *anyone* know what squadron this is?"

At 0900, the gong and the bos'n's pipe call us to General Quarters. A few minutes later we pass through the net and head for the open sea. Our three carriers fall into line astern of us. Two battleships follow them, and the light cruisers take station on our flanks. Their camouflage is excellent. Near as the cruisers are, it's almost impossible to tell whether they're opening or closing the distance.

The ships we have left at anchor are already an indistinguishable blur, except for the dazzling white of a hospital ship. As we steady onto our course, the sun glares from the huge, freshly-painted "10" on the forward end of our flight deck. A sharp breeze is blowing. There are rainbows in the spray. Big red flying fish curvet across our bows.

A battery of 20-mm guns is just below the starboard side of flag bridge. One of the gunners is singing, "We're off to see the Wizard, the wonderful Wizard of Oz!"

February 11th (Sunday). At sea

Shortly after dawn the temperature in our room was 94°. Fans and blowers can't combat this kind of heat. You have to sleep on your bottom sheet until it gets soaked and wakes you up, then strip it back and sleep on your top sheet. I bought a dollar's worth of air mail stamps on the way to church and tucked them in my shirt pocket. When I took them out, an hour later, they were hopelessly glued together.

Protestant services were held in the after messing compartment, on the third deck. The tables had been shoved aside, and the steel benches ranked like pews. One table was the altar; it held a cross and two candlesticks, standing on a red velvet cloth, fringed, and embroidered in gold, "HOLY HOLY HOLY." In front of the altar was a microphone. A lectern holding a blue leather Bible with gold lettering, "U.S.S. Yorktown," stood at the left. At the right was a miniature organ.

These were the only trappings of religion. Everything else in the compartment was an implement of war. The organist's stool was the crate for the tail of a 500-pound bomb. The bulkheads were lined with worktables where rockets are prepared for loading. On one bulkhead was this sign: "Notice! No smoking while explosives are stored here." Cases of am-

19

munition were stacked under the benches. And every few minutes the service was interrupted by some such announcement as "Now the Gunnery Officer please dial 222," or "Now the fifth division man Bomb Supply Forward."

The chaplain, George Wright, once interrupted himself: "What's the matter with you men? Your faces are so long this morning, you could eat oatmeal out of an 8-inch pipe!"

The matter wasn't hard to guess. We all knew we were headed for Tokyo. Or maybe some other married men's prayer books happened to open, as mine did, at this verse from the 63rd Psalm: "I remember thee upon my bed and meditate on thee in the night watches."

Still, there's this to be said for fleet duty: you never pick up a glass and find its rim smeared with lipstck.

February 12th. At sea

This morning the air group staged a show. One of our light cruisers, the *Biloxi,* streamed a spar on a long line, and our F6Fs chopped it to splinters with their guns. When you watch a strafing run, you experience a curious dislocation of the normal time sequence. Somehow you expect to see and hear the shot, then see and hear the splash. Actually, you see the shot, see the splash, then hear the shot and hear the splash. A .50-caliber burst sounds like ripping heavy canvas, but the bullets hit the water and a muffled *frrrrrrrp!*

Two of our fighters collided as they peeled off, and locked together. Both pilots jumped, but only one parachute opened. Six of the rest had landed when the bull horn announced, "The plane now coming in will make landing number 19,000." It was an F6F, number 5. Two bakers were standing by with a big cake for the pilot, and a photographer took his picture, to add to the series posted in the wardroom.

In the afternoon, the gunnery department worked out on a sleeve towed by a TBM. My God, how I hate those 5-inch guns! If I had the choice of standing on the bridge of a battleship during a 16-inch broadside, or on a carrier's bridge while the 5-inchers were firing, I'd take the 16-inchers every time. Their concussion is tremendous, but it builds up. It's like being hit by a slow truck wrapped in sofa cushions. The 5-inchers, damn them, hit you like a plank. They're especially rough when you're on flag bridge. There, when Number 2 mount trains abeam, the muzzles are only 25 feet away, and the blast jolts your teeth loose. You don't mind it so much when they're firing at an enemy plane; your excitement and anxiety insulate you. But when it's nothing but target practice, your attention wraps itself right around the gun barrels, and you feel every concussion to its uttermost erg. I'll never get used to them. Like Petruchio's horse, I'm simply "past cure of the fives."

I was working in my room this afternoon when the public address system announced. "Stand by for a starboardside run!" I heard the whine of turrets turning, and presently BLAM! The plug on the electric fan cord jumped out of its socket. A photograph fell over. The glasses rattled in their racks, and dust sifted down from the overhead. Then the 40-mms came on, with a rhythm like a trolley car with a flat wheel. Then the little 20s started hiccoughing. The ventilating system sucked up their acrid smoke and blew it into the room. That was the end. I went topside, as mad as if all this had been done for my personal discomfiture.

February 13th. At sea

The wise took oil in their vessels.

This morning was our last chance to fuel before the strike. We came alongside our tanker under reduced speed—she's the *Cacapon*, 25,000 tons— passed her our hawsers and phone lines, and began to drag her hoses across. The sea was glassy, but we were headed into a long, rolling swell that made both ships pitch heavily. The hoses, hanging from the tall yards, threshed back and forth. Hauling a hose from one ship to another is like hauling a boa constrictor out of a tree. It writhes and clings and jerks with live resistance, and even after it has been made fast to the intake pipe, it struggles to break away.

We fueled from the tanker's port side, of course, so I could look straight down at her from flag bridge. Her flanks were dripping with weeds, bright green ones. They rose and fell with the swells, and when the noon sun struck them through the blue water, they became iridescent, like a pigeon's throat or a peacock's tail.

Presently the *Washington* came up on her starboard side. As she made fast, one of the signalmen told me, "Look there, sir—just under her Number 2 turret."

It was a fox terrier, wearing a red life preserver around his neck. Compared with a carrier, a battleship has a low freeboard, and the swells rushing through the narrow channel between the *Washington* and the *Cacapon* were squeezed up until they towered deck-high. As the crest of each swell swept past, the terrier chased it, barking, until it was amidships. Then he'd leave it and trot back to chase the next. In a few minutes, the *Washington* struck her nose deeper than usual. Green water broke over her fo'c'sle and sloshed down her deck. The terrier saw it just in time. He fled under the turret and stayed there.

The *Washington* looks like a smart ship. The Admiral must have thought so too, because when she took in her lines, hauled down Baker, and stood away, he ordered our signal bridge to fly Baker, Pennant 5, Pennant 6. Tare, Victor, George —"Well done, *Washington!*"

That's a nice signal to receive, but I agree with Mueck, the flag's Chief Signalman, that the best hoist of all is Fox Charlie Dog—"Cease present exercises." From there, we fell to talking about the What-the-hell pennant. Mueck had never seen one, and the only one I ever saw was being used as a decoration in the O club at Havannah, on Efate—a black pennant with three red asterisks, three yellow question marks, and three green exclamation points. I've been told that a squadron commander or a task group commander flies it when one of his subordinate commanders has done something particularly stupid.

The flag signalmen—Wolfe, Buck, Shorty, Red, and the rest—are a sharp bunch of youngsters. They take the fastest blinkers in their stride, and although we've got sixteen destroyers in our screen, virtually indistinguishable from one another as far as I'm concerned, the boys need only a glance to identify them.

Chief Mueck—"rhymes with 'Buick,'" Hendy said when he introduced us—wears steel-rimmed spectacles, which increase his resemblance to a young gospel-shouter, but I have a feeling that the burthen of Mueck's shouts would be unbecoming to a pulpit.

The only other man on flag bridge is Chief Quartermaster Jones, a small, tough, brisk, Scottie-type, with a soft voice and a tuneless whistle. Jones is probably the senior of the lot, and I doubt if he's more than twenty-five or -six.

This afternoon I had coffee in the wardroom with a couple of torpedo pilots. One said, "You know, I think all this coffee is keeping me awake."

"Not me," the other said. "It's not the jamoke. What's keeping *me* awake is Tokyo!"

February 14th. At sea

Today is Ash Wednesday, so it's a convenient time for me to stop smoking. If I don't, I'm not sure I can make it from my room to my battle station on the double-double, as I'll have to do when the fight begins. I ran a time trial this morning, combined with a "terrain familiarization hop," as pilots call it. Here's the course, beginning at my room on the second deck:

Run forward about seventy-five feet and up the ladder to the hangar deck, then run aft about twenty feet and up two ladders to the gallery deck; run forward twenty feet, up a ladder to the flight deck, up another to the first superstructure deck, and up another to flag bridge—six (*puff!*) steep (*wheeze!*) ladders (*cough!*). Result: the Anti-Tobacco League gets a new member, as of today.

Flag bridge hangs on the forward end of the island, 315 feet from the bow, 545 feet from the stern, and 80 feet above the waterline. It is a narrow, horseshoe-shaped balcony about five feet wide at the toe, tapering to three feet along the shanks. Steel plating four feet high runs around its outer edge. This plate isn't thick enough to stop anything heavier than a .50-caliber bullet, if that; but at least it will keep you from falling off the bridge. It also serves as a mount for the speaking tubes that lead into flag plot, and for the flag signalmen's searchlights and telescopes.

Flag plot, which flag bridge encloses on three sides, is the Admiral's battle headquarters. Just as Captain Combs's battle headquarters—the pilothouse, on the next level above—is the nerve center of the ship, flag plot is the nerve center of the task group. All battle information funnels through this cramped room. Radiomen rush in with sheaves of fresh dispatches. Coded messages to and from other commands rasp over TBS. A red light flashes on the squawk-box, and air plot makes its report. Returned pilots stumble up from their planes, sweating under their heavy flight gear, and tell the Admiral what they have seen and done. Signalmen bring in the messages they have just taken down from blinker or semaphore. Through the speaking tubes come the ghostly voices of the observers outside on flag bridge. A desk phone, or a Marine orderly, or an Intelligence officer brings more news. Still more comes from needles, dials, pin-point lights: the compass; the speed log; the anemometer, reporting the velocity and relative direction of the wind; the DRT—Dead Reckoning Tracer, also

23

known as "the bug"—automatically plotting the ship's course; the PPI scope—Plan Position Indicator—reflecting the positions of the ships around us.

Men have to watch these instruments. The information that some of them record has to be logged. Chief Quartermaster Jones and the duty quartermaster guard "the bug" and keep the flag plot log. An officer with earphones plots the positions of all airborne planes, as relayed by CIC—the Combat Information Center. The staff duty officer stands by the TBS, and a yeoman types down every word it carries, incoming or outgoing. Behind a heavy curtain, a radarman hunches over his scope.

All these instruments and the men in charge of them, all their plotting boards and desks and chairs, their files and typewriters and reference books, are jammed into a room half the size of a squash court. From six to eight staff officers are also there, and an orderly or two. Traffic streams in and out. Lights flash, bells ring, whistles shrill, loudspeakers mumble and shout. Yet it is here, in this relentless uproar and confusion, that the battle is planned and fought.

Flag plot has two doors, one leading to the port side of flag bridge, the other to the starboard side; they are baffle-doors; no light can get past them. It also has six ports, but steel plates are dogged over them at night and during battle, so the men within can't see anything for themselves; everything they learn, they learn at second hand; something or somebody passes them the word—one of the "somebodies," the Admiral tells me, being me. I'm to man the portside speaking tube.

Good! We haven't got much protection out on the bridge, but we won't have to wait to be told when to duck.

The Plan of the Day ends, "Tokyo bound. Starting today, all personnel will keep sleeves rolled down and shirts buttoned. Officers will wear medical kits. No sun-bathing, no athletics. Place flameproof mattress covers on mattresses."

February 15th. At sea

Cooper Bright hasn't improved at all in the six months since I last saw him. The fact is, he's worse. In those days, he spent only about half his time devising ribs and insults; now he seems to work three eight-hour shifts a day. If he can make a victim mad, Coop is happy. If he can scare him,

24

he is happier. If he can make him mad and scare him at the same time, he's happiest of all.

This morning Coop slipped a harpoon into the air group. Coop comes from New Jersey, and professes to regard all Southerners with the same contemptuous distaste as Admiral Halsey has for the Japanese. Unfortunately for the South, he has access to air plot's teletypewriter, which prints its messages in the four ready rooms and the Air Combat Intelligence office, so his slurs automatically get wide publicity. One of our fighter pilots is named Robert E. Lee. Here is what he, and every other Southerner in the air group, was slapped in the face with today: "AND SO WE SANG THE CHORUS FROM ATLANTA TO THE SEA, AS WE GO MARCHING THROUGH GEORGIA"—DEDICATED TO ROBERT E. LEE OF VF 3.

Coop may make them mad, but they're grateful to him. His nonsense takes their minds off more lively troubles.

Contact!—trivial, but our first. This morning two Hellcats strafed and sank a small Jap boat. The destroyer *Hailey* was sent over to look for survivors, and the one she found was put aboard us tonight. Prisoners are usually confined in the brig, but this one was taken to sick bay because his leg had been smashed by a bullet during the strafing. The staff Japanese language officer, Bill Kluss, went down to interrogate him and told me about it later.

The Jap was seventeen years old, Bill said, a nice, clean-looking kid. His wound must have been painful, but he never stopped smiling through the whole interview. It began with the stock questions: Name? Sadao Watanabe. Home? Choshi, on Honshu. Officer or enlisted man? The boy said, "I do not understand."

"Aren't you in the Navy? Wasn't that a picket boat you were in?"

"No. I am a fisherman."

"Then what were you doing 400 miles from land?"

The boy said that he and ten other fishermen had put to sea twenty-nine days before. They were only two miles offshore when their engine failed, and they had drifted ever since, living on rain water and fish.

At this point in the story, Bill said, a corpsman put a tray of chow on the boy's knees, and two peas rolled off into the bed-clothes. Bill said the boy's ribs looked like a xylophone, but before he took a single mouthful, he hunted for those peas and put them back on his plate—he was *that* hungry. Bill

25

let him finish his meal, then asked, "What happened to the other ten men?"

"They were killed when the Emperor's planes attacked our boat this morning."

"When *whose* planes attacked you?"

"The Emperor's. We didn't understand it, but we had been told that China had no planes."

Bill was puzzled. Presently he asked, "Do you think Japan will win the war?"

"Certainly. China is big, but she is weak."

"Look, Sadao," Bill said. "Where do you think you are now?"

"I don't know. All I know is that I am with friends."

When the real situation was explained to him, he wasn't alarmed or even abashed. On the contrary, he announced that as soon as his leg was healed, he would like to enlist in the United States Navy and spend the rest of his life with his wonderful new friends.

Telling me about it, Bill asked, "How the hell can you dope out people like that?"

February 16th. At sea

All day today Task Force 58 sent its planes against Tokyo. The early morning was still wet and black when the *Yorktown* launched her first strike, and a wet night was falling when she landed her last one. Our pilots flew off and fought, returned for food and fuel, and flew off and fought again. I heard them briefed in their ready rooms, went to flag bridge to watch them take off and land, and returned to the ready rooms to hear them interrogated. I remember very little of what they accomplished, but I remember how they looked and what they said.

The morning began around 0500 in Ready 2, where the fighters were checking over their flight gear and taking down last-minute information from the ticker screen. Considering the nature of their mission, the virtual certainty of heavy interception and thick AA over the target, and the probability of day-long attacks on the ship, everyone was surprisingly cool. I mentioned this to McLeroy: "Not much excitement, is there? It's like any day in any ready room."

Mac said, "Hell, it's too late to get excited now. The time to get excited is just before you join the Navy."

Some of the pilots were discussing the weather, which

26

was foul. One said, "We've only got a 300-foot ceiling outside. It'll be better over Tokyo, though. At least, that's what I keep telling myself...."

Just then the teletype started chattering, and a message tripped across the screen: FLYING CONDITIONS UNDESIRABLE.

A pilot jerked his thumb toward it: "That means the ceiling is below the waterline. I hope they got gills on these airy-o-planes."

Another said, "Ceiling zero, Dodgers five."

The ticker chattered again: FROM CAPTAIN COMBS —THIS IS THE DAY WE HAVE BEEN WAITING FOR. YOU ALL KNOW YOUR JOB AND I KNOW YOU WILL DO IT WITH THE SAME OUTSTANDING RESULTS YOU HAVE OBTAINED IN THE PAST. STICK TOGETHER, TEAM, AND GIVE THEM THE WORKS. WE WILL KEEP THE FIGHTING LADY READY FOR YOUR RETURN. There was a pause, then one line more: THE POOR LITTLE AIR OFFICER SAYS GIVE THEM HELL.

Just before the first strike was called, Fighting 3's skipper, Fritz Wolfe, picked up the microphone. "Another thing. If you have to make a forced landing, I suggest you make it in Lake Kasumigaura. It'll give you time to cool off. If you land on the ground, you may be picked up by civilians. However, it's your plane, so do what you want with it."

The ticker printed, PILOTS MAN YOUR AIR BUGGIES, and they ran up to the dark deck. I was leaving for flag bridge when the air group's Flight Surgeon, Doc Voris, came down the passageway and asked if I'd seen our prisoner.

"Not yet. I'm going down today or tomorrow."

"Be sure to catch him at mealtime. It's a sight for your whiskers. This morning he went through two full trays like a turpentined mare through a five-bar gate."

The first of the F6F's was taxiing into position as I reached the bridge. Its engine roared louder and louder. Suddenly the plane jumped forward and into the air, and all I could see was its dwindling lights. Another plane followed it, and another and another. Soon the deafening deck was silent again, and there was nothing to do but wait for them to return.

Around 0715, the radio in air plot stated, "We've got plenty of work in the next half-hour." None of us recognized the voice, but we knew it was some pilot on his way to the target. Nick Cline, assistant Operations, said fervently, "Plenty of work, and you ain't kidding, bud!"

A couple of hours later, there was a rumor that the first

strike was lost in the weather, but that the second strike was breaking out of the overcast, slapping down the enemy, and ducking back into the overcast. No one on the ship really knew what was happening until 1100, when the first strike landed. The pilots came down to their ready rooms and all of them talked at once, while they shucked off their gear and yelled for sandwiches and coffee.

"Everywhere I looked, there were these goddam bi-planes. *Bi*-planes! The wily Jape must be scraping the bottom of his goddam barrel!"

"Konoike had planes all over the field, and not a son of a bitch near 'em. We caught 'em with their pants down!"

"Goddam Phantom planes flew under us and fouled up our run!" ("Phantom" is the call-sign for the air group from another carrier.)

"Japan is nowhere near as pretty as Formosa. Did you see those sand dunes, and the snow on the mountains?"

"Mine didn't flame till the last burst. It hit his port engine, and VOOM!"

"I was chasing this Oscar, and the pilot jumped out with no chute. Son of a bitch hit the ground and *bounced,* so help my Christ! I was so busy watching him, I didn't watch the Oscar, and goddam if it didn't make a shallow turn and pull straight up into me. I fired, and it crashed and burst into pieces.

"Damn Phantom planes dropping their belly-tanks, and coming at you just like Tojos!"

"I caught him in a split-S and just sawed him to pieces. The bastard must have been dead already, because he attacked us with his wheels down. I thought it was a Val at first." (A Val is an obsolete Jap dive bomber with fixed landing gear.)

"Who was in 65? He was all the hell over the sky!"

And so on, all day long.

About half the fighters on the second strike had landed when the bull horn warned us, "The next plane coming in is severely damaged. Heads up on the flight deck!"

The F6F came up the groove smoothly and settled down to a perfect landing. As it taxied past flag bridge, I saw that ten or twelve square feet of its port wing, including the whole aileron, had been shot away.

There was a lull at 1400, so I stopped by air plot. Cooper Bright was sitting in a desk drawer, like an oversized Kayo. The Air officer, Comdr. Myron T. Evans, was dozing on the transom. The radio was tuned to Tokyo, and Doctor

28

Somebody-or-Other was discussing America's manpower problem.

"The United States has only 1,000,000 men to work its factories," he said. "Every month 100,000 men and women are deserting the war effort. They realize, as does the American Navy, that carrier-based aircraft do not dare come within range of our land-based aircraft, and that——"

Right here the Doctor was cut off the air, and a new voice made this announcement: "An attack by carrier planes is now going on. We have been watching their surface forces for many days, and even now our land-based planes are rising to administer punishment. The purpose of this attack is revenge for our recent destruction of Amrican B-29s. Out of 60 B-29s, we shot down 17. One Japanese fighter plane has not yet returned."

"Empty," Evans said, "I wouldn't sit up for it, Mac!"

When the results of the day's strikes were tabulated, it appeared that the four air groups in this task group had destroyed 63 Jap planes in the air and 45 more on the ground. The figures sound big, but everybody agrees that the interception was far lighter than expected, in view of the fact that we were attacking the area where most of the planes in the Empire are concentrated.

Jim Smith said, "The explanation is perfectly simple. It means that the Jap high command is exactly like ours. The closer you get to headquarters, the harder it is to get anything done. You have to go through channels, and sweat your way up the chain of command, and when you've made six copies of everything, some un-retired admiral sends them back because you dropped a comma. If we'd been attacking an island outpost today, a tough Reserve lieutenant would have seen us coming and thrown all his planes into the air, and there'd have been one hell of a fight.

"But headquarters doesn't do things that way. The order to intercept us is probably waiting for some admiral's signature right now, and the admiral is out playing golf."

February 17th. At sea

The fleet always stands General Quarters for the hour before dawn and the hour after dusk, since these are the most probable times for an attack. A gong rings, a bugle blows, and the bos'n's mate of the watch calls, "General quarters! General quarters! Man your battle stations!" The sleeping ship springs awake, and men rush through the passageways and up the ladders, buttoning their trousers, zipping their jackets, and rubbing drowsiness from their eyes. A few minutes later the night is silent again, but this is a different silence. It is a jungle silence, alert and menacing.

A wet wind poured across flag bridge at General Quarters this morning. Low, scudding clouds screened the whole sky. Once a single star broke through briefly; the guns of Number 3 mount swung up and clamped on it while it shone, then swung down, waiting. At first the planes on the flight deck were dim blurs. Gradually they solidified, until I could distinguish the F6Fs.

The assistant Air officer, "Pappy" Harshman, picked up his microphone. The bull horn magnified his voice to a bellow: "Prepare to start engines! . . . Stand clear of propellers! . . . Start engines!"

The starter cartridges hissed and fizzed, but only three engines exploded into power; the weather had numbed the rest. Crewmen had to "wind them up," laboriously tugging the heavy propellers around to build up compression in the cylinders. One engine after another finally came to life, until all were coughing and backfiring except the fighter on the port catapult and one in the front rank. These stayed dead. Plane-handling crews shoved them onto Number 1 elevator and sent them below. The gaps they left were filled before the elevator returned.

A flight deck ready for a predawn take-off is like a cross section of the bottommost level of hell: black, cold and roaring. The thunder of the engines shakes the ship. Pale blue flames flicker from their exhausts and are reflected from the wet deck, until the propellers blast the puddles dry. Like pit imps, the taxi crews brandish red and green flashlights as they guide the pilots into takeoff position. At such a time, you can almost taste the danger that saturates the deck. Tolerances on a live flight deck are always small, but now they are infinitesimal. An instant's inattention, a slip or even a lurch, an extravagant gesture, a languid response, and a man loses a limb or his life to those murderous propellers. No actuary on earth could list all the ways that you can get killed or maimed on a live flight deck. I once saw a crewman standing just in front of an SBD's port wing, where the Pitot tube sticks out like a lance tip. The pilot of the plane ahead suddenly gunned his engine, the crewman was blown off balance, and the Pitot tube tore his ear and gouged his check.

The first strike landed at 1030, and I went down to the ready rooms to hear the pilots' stories. The men trooped in, some of them shouting with excitement, others dumb with exhaustion. Their wet gear dripped pools on the deck while they slanted their hands and made the moaning noises that always go with a description of maneuvers:

"I got some slugs in one, but I blacked out in the middle of it. I don't know what happened to him."

"He must have hit the tail. I wasn't shooting at *him*, I was shooting at the plane. He must have had a spring in his chute, because it popped right open, and he was hanging in it, dead."

"They're crazy! They cluster around a plane on the ground, and you go down and strafe them, and they scatter, and you do a wing-over, and they're right back at the plane again."

"Fujiyama was beautiful, but Tokyo looked like Hong-kong, only bigger and browner. It looked like part of the earth—reckon it was camouflaged? Anyhow, it's not like any city at home: no big buildings at all. All the reservoirs were frozen, and there was snow everywhere. I'd hate like hell to go down in that country!"

Pray ye that your flight be not in the winter ...

The second strike brought home another cripple today. "Heads up!" the bull horn said. "The next man coming in has no tail hook!"

The plane was F6F Number 2, with a pilot named Reitel. He made a beautiful landing, but his brakes wouldn't hold on the wet surface, and he plowed into the wire barrier at 70 knots. The plane tipped up on its nose, the prop gouged chunks out of the deck, and Reitel pitched forward in his straps, his arms flailing. Then the plane fell back, and he climbed out unhurt. *Yet lives our pilot still. ...*

The Landing Signals officer, Dick Tripp, invited me aft to his little platform to watch the third strike return, around noon. He brought them in smoothly, plane after plane, with hardly a wave-off. In fact, his expert teamwork with the pilots became monotonous. But suddenly, as an SB2C's tail hook caught, something fell from its belly and split apart, and the prop-wash blew a white blizzard over the whole after end of the flight deck.

Dick's assistant, Lee Spaulding, said, "Must be shedding their tail feathers."

They turned out to be propaganda leaflets. The pilot had

tried to drop them over Japan, but they had hung up until the shock of landing jarred them loose.

Carl Ballinger, the flag Fighter Director officer, bet that the Japs would trail our strikes home to the task force today and work us over with *kamikazes*. When General Quarters blared out at 1600, everybody thought that Carl would collect. False alarm. We secured a few minutes later.

Radiotokyo got on its hip with an opium pipe and dreamed up this one tonight:

"American carrier-borne aircraft under command of Admiral Marc A. Mitscher continued strikes in and around the Tokyo area Saturday, but the attackers failed to cause any serious damage. Preliminary estimates showed that Japanese fliers and antiaircraft batteries shot down 147 enemy planes and damaged 50 others. In assaults against the large carrier task force, one cruiser was sunk and another large American warship, believed to have been a carrier, was seriously damaged and burned from our attacks. Other damage was done to sundry other American warships."

No, brother! No, no, *no!* It's too soon for us to file an affidavit on exactly how many planes the strikes yesterday and today have cost the task force; all the figures aren't in yet. But taking the *Yorktown's* air group as an average, the total losses won't be more than a dozen, if that many. Air Group 3 has lost one plane—that's all. Frank Onion got hopped yesterday, had a finger shot off, and took some bullets in his engine. His plane ditched and sank, but Frank himself is back aboard the ship already.

And as for a cruiser being sunk and a carrier damaged —apcray!

February 18th (Sunday). At sea

An easy day today. Except for routine dawn and dusk General Quarters, we weren't turned out but once, at 2215, and then the bogeys proved to be a flight of B-29s returning from Japan.

Afterwards, I stopped by Pat Patterson's room. "Doing anything, Pat?"

"Not a thing. Come on in. I'm just sittin' aroun', wishin' I could go ashore and get me a drink."

I said, "You have described my naval career."

Pat said, "We'll get ashore together one o' these days. You got to play in one of our 'limination contests."

"Never heard of them. How do they work?"

"Well, one time when we were at the Bremerton Yard we had one, an' I got through the list twicet an' was startin' on the third time aroun' when they shut up the place. Didn't cost me a cent; the owner paid for the whole thing. Know what I mean?—the list over the bar. They have 'em everywhere. They always start off the same: Scotch an' water, Scotch an' soda, bourbon an' water, bourbon an' soda, then dry Martini an' Tom Collins, Daiquiri an' so on. They had twenty-two drinks on this here one, an' like I told you, I was on my third time aroun' when they told me to stop. I said 'You gonna shut up the bar?'

"He said—that's the man who owned it—'I sure am.'

"I said, 'Please, mister, will you gimme a double Scotch an' soda to get home on?' He give it to me, too. Never cost me a cent."

February 19th. At sea. L-Day at Iwo Jima

I had it all fixed to hitch-hike a ride in an SB2C on the first strike this morning, but the Air officer killed it at the last minute. It would have been a great sight, this landing. The only one I ever watched was at Empress Augusta Bay, on Bougainville, on November 1, 1943. I was in a TBF then. We circled the beachhead at 500 feet for nearly two hours. but we might as well have stood in bed. The jungle swallowed the troops as soon as they stepped ashore. Iwo Jima is small and bare. The whole business would have been right under my eyes.

Next best thing to actually watching an operation is following it over the radio. Air plot's was tuned to the frequency used by the spotting officer, who is supposed to hover close to the ground in his little Cub and mark the targets for the strike planes. By the time I got to air plot, two spotters had already been shot down, and the third one—call-sign "Grady"—seemed reluctant to tempt the Japs' AA again.

His controller, the air-ground co-ordinator, kept urging him to go lower, so that he could see better, but Grady's only reply was, "Can't promise anything, but I'll do the best I can."

The quaver in his voice was so plain, Cooper Bright said, "Sounds like a political appointee."

The Navigator, Comdr. "Jesse" James, seldom misses a

chance to smack a slapstick over Coop's shining scalp. Whenever he catches Coop without a cap, he tells him, "Cover up, will you, Bright? I've taken two sights on your head already." Late this afternoon Coop and I were catching a breath on the flight deck, when Jesse yelled down from the pilothouse, "Sunset! Darken ship! Get that cap on!"

Scraps: On most ships, the junior officers' bunkroom is called "the Junkroom." The *Yorktown* calls it "Boys Town."

The Air Combat Intelligence office is crowded with cartons of propaganda leaflets. For reasons known best to the high command, they are classified "Secret." Back at the Navy Department, I once saw a reproduction of a photograph which a Jap pilot had snapped over Pearl Harbor on December 7, 1941. It had been clipped from a Jap magazine and had been classified "Confidential."

One of our mess attendants has the curious name of Poogey. On the *Lex* we had one named General Napoleon and another named Love Kisses Love.

February 20th. At sea

I was in flag plot this afternoon when one of our destroyers —TBS call sign "Tortoise"—reported a sound contact with a submarine, and began dropping depth charges. He wasn't having much success, so the screen commander—call sign "Russia 4"—asked if he wanted help.

Tortoise's "Negative!" was positive. In a few minutes he began dropping depth charges again, but still with no luck. The screen commander waited a while, then ordered another of his dstroyers to join the hunt: "Sweetheart, this is Russia 4. Assist Tortoise in sound contact."

Sweetheart, bursting with eagerness, shouted "Wilco!", and bucketed over toward Tortoise. We all went out to flag bridge to watch them. They quartered the area and combed it, but they couldn't raise the sub.

Another pleasure of fleet duty, in addition to no lipstick on the cups and glasses: I haven't seen a fly or an insect of any sort since we put to sea.

February 21st. At sea

When the first strike took off this morning, one of the fighters cut across the starboard corner of the ramp, and a gunner there ducked his head just in time. As one of the TBMs trundled down the deck, a hand appeared in the tunnel port, thumbs up.

None of our planes wears any identification whatsoever, except its number. Sometimes all the planes in a squadron will display a small emblem, about the size of a saucer, but I have yet to see a Navy plane bedizened with circus posters like the Army's. One reason, of course, is that a Navy pilot has no personal plane of his own; he may fly a different plane on each of a dozen successive missions. But the basic reason, I think, is that Navy pilots simply don't care for the 24-sheet school of decoration.

Most of the Marine orderlies aboard use comic books and picture magazines to pass their long waits between errands, but the Exec has an orderly who reads the New Testament and underlines passages with a red pencil.

Time out this morning for a quick rubber of bridge in Ready 2 with Joe Mayer, Fritz Wolfe and Peter Grace. The "Vulture for Culture," as Joe calls himself, kept complaining that the rest of us jabbered so much, he couldn't concentrate on the game. Fritz said, "When the *kamikazes* come over, I suppose you'll want the AA to lay off while you figure out what to lead, hey?"

Whereupon Joe, completely rattled, led the king of trumps from dummy and played the ace from his own hand.

"Sharp!" Fritz told him. "Plenty sharp, boy! Wouldn't let dummy get by with *that* finesse, would you?"

About midafternoon, we had our first sight of land since we left Ulithi eleven days ago: the sugar-loaf mountain of Kita Iwo Jima. Suddenly a huge school of porpoises, hundreds of them, broke water on our port bow and stitched across the surface in pace with the ship. The air group's Flight Surgeon, Doc Voris, and I watched their caracoles for perhaps twenty minutes. That night the two of us were going to have dinner in the chief petty officers' mess, and I told him, "No matter how we exaggerate these porpoises, I bet that some chief will have a topper."

Sure enough, when we mentioned seeing them, a Chief Gunner's Mate asked, "How big did you say they were, sir? About six feet long? Well, I mind one day off Amoy we saw some—nineteen feet long if they were an inch, and bright pink. You can strike me—"

Air Defense! There were seven ladders to climb instead

35

of six, and by the time I reached flag bridge, the task group off to port was already in action. Its 5-inch guns were flickering, and red chains of 40s were climbing the sky. An instant later, our own 5-inchers cut, loose, firing straight across the flight deck. The noise was so shattering, I felt like a chump from Chumpsville when I reported through the speaking tube, "Our 5-inch batteries have opened fire."

They stopped after a few minutes, and there was no sound but the clang of the empty cartridge cases rolling about the flight deck. When the smoke and sparks had blown away, a plane crew ran out to look at a night-fighter F6F which was parked almost directly under the muzzles of Number 1 mount. The pilot was deaf and dizzy; he crawled out of his cockpit, shaking his head, and stumbled into flight deck control.

We secured, but scuttlebutt said it wouldn't be for long. It wasn't. I had gone down to my room and was pulling on heavy clothes against the cold drizzle when General Quarters sounded. By now it was dark, except for a half-moon dead overhead. The twin 5-inch guns looked, in the dim light, like two toothpicks stuck in a cocktail canapé. The *Randolph* and some of our destroyers fired a few rounds, but our guns didn't open. While we waited for "secure," Mueck and I fell to discussing the first drink we'd have when we got back to San Francisco.

Stew Lindsay came down from the comm office and told me, "Well, the old *Sara* got it. Three *kamikazes* smacked her."

I'm sorry for two reasons, the second one selfish: the *Sara* is so tremendous, she was certain to draw the attack. Now that she's left the task force, they'll hit the *Essexes*.

February 22nd. At sea

The Exec put the whole text of the Gettysburg Address in his Plan of the Day for the 12th, but today he didn't mention George Washington.

Our only fresh news comes from the four-page Radio Press, which is distributed at breakfast every morning. Sometimes it reads as if George Ade were the editor: "Russian Troops threatening to turn Berlin's Eastern Defenses along the Oder River have fought their way into the Walled Medieval town of Guben, key communications center 51 miles Southeast of the Reich Capital."

I can usually figure out the misprints and garbles, but there's one in this morning's news that defeats me: "Moscow and other Continental sources reported distardels in bomb-blackened Dresden and other Saxony Towns." *Distardels?* Disturbances?

If I ever had any doubt about the muzzle-blast of a 5-inch gun, I haven't now. This morning I stopped by the hangar deck to see what Number 1 mount had done to that F6F-N last night. Well, the glass in its canopy was shattered, its longerons were bent, its skin crumpled, its ribs twisted, and its rivets sheared. A TBM, too, had been blasted, by the after mounts. All its glass was broken, including its starboard wingtip light. Sheets of its skin were flapping as if they'd never been riveted at all. The ribs in the flipper were sprung, the fabric was torn, and the rudder was completely collapsed.

Both planes were ruined beyond repair. There was nothing to do but cannibalize their instruments and engines, and throw the skeletons over the side.

Cold weather doesn't help my heat rash as much as I had hoped. After a shower tonight, my back, arms, and legs felt as if they were on fire. Somebody suggested that I stop using soap. I'd stop washing altogether, if it would help any.

February 23rd. At sea

At a target angle of about 30°, a battleship looks as speedy as a PT boat. We were changing course this morning when I happened to glance at the *Washington*, astern of us. It may have been the low clouds that caused the illusion, but I'd have sworn she was making 60 knots.

The destroyer *Craven* came under our port quarter to transfer a TBM crew back to the *San Jacinto*. A day or so ago, their engine had conked when they were a half-hour on their way to Tokyo, and they had gone in the drink. The destroyer *Hazlewood* had fished them out and put them aboard us, and now they were going home. As the *Craven* stood in, I saw a Jap flag and a slant painted on her bridge. The flag meant, of course, that she had shot down a Jap plane, but the slant was new to me. Someone thought it meant that she had exploded a mine.

When the lines were passed and secured, the *Craven* sent across a bos'n's chair. A heavy sea was running, and the chair jumped and danced. The torpedo pilot watched it gloomily:

37

"They should have given me my choice of a last breakfast."

He climbed in and started back, his head bumping the line. One of our bos'n's mates chanted him across: "Slack off! . . . Heave, sailors! . . . Up on it! . . . Take it in! . . . Heave, now! . . . Up on it, sailors! . . . Slack off, now! . . . Easy . . . *Easy!*"

The last crewman climbed out of the chair, and the lines were taken in. The First Lieutenant, Comdr. John W. Brady, called through his megaphone. "Thank you!", then told his talker, "All lines are clear."

The *Craven* sprinted away.

We fueled from the tanker *Marias* this morning at the same time as the *Biloxi*. The cruiser had hardly drawn even with us when she started blinking as frantically as if it were an SOS. I asked a signalman what she was saying. He watched the flashes for a moment: "She wants to know if we have any movies to exchange."

The *Marias'* camouflage was streaked and battered. I can't imagine why they even try to disguise a tanker. She couldn't possibly be mistaken for anything else. Four Jap flags are painted on the *Biloxi's* bridge, and three Jap ships. It's nice to know she's got a good gun team aboard.

While we fueled, the ships' signalmen semaphored back and forth, as usual. Their economy of gesture is fascinating to watch. They don't use flags, or even their arms—just their hands, and they flip them at an unbelievable rate. Veteran signalmen tell me they can always cross up a novice by sending him the word *redredge,* and spacing it this way: *red-red-ge.* Another of their tricks is *Manila milkman.* Sending it, you can put your right hand at the *A* position and keep it there through the whole phrase.

There was a violent argument in Ready 1 this afternoon. One pilot was contending that Tom Rover had married Dora Stanhope, while another said that Dora had married Dick. Of course! Tom's girl was Nellie Laning.

Two new cartoons on the wardroom bulletin board tonight. The first had been clipped from a magazine. It showed a grotesque carrier (cartoonists must live in caves) with a base-ball game being played on the flight deck. In the foreground is an equally grotesque plane, with the radioman telling the pilots tell their story in pantomime. Passing the bridge, they inning." Under the caption, some disgruntled pilot had written, "Might as well. We always do."

The other cartoon was a local production. It showed George Earnshaw peeking out of a 5-inch mount at two wrecked planes on the flight deck. Caption: "Three more, and I'll be an ace!"

February 24th. At sea

We topped off our destroyers this morning in a sea still so heavy that the little cans bucked and twisted like mustangs. Once the hoses tore loose, and brown oil gushed over the foam between us. Even the big *Yorktown* was pitching. Spindrift whistled over the bow and stung us on the bridge. Just as one of our TBMs took off, the sun made a perfect rainbow dead ahead of us, and the plane flew through its center. I half-expected huge letters to appear: THE END.

Waves as high as these turn our flight deck into a seesaw that swings through an arc of 20 feet or more. A pilot will bring his plane in to a perfect landing, only to have the deck fall away from him or rise and smash him from below. He can't wait for a favorable moment; he has to bore in at a steady speed and take his chances. An F6F from the *Randolph* came aboard us this afternoon as a particularly high sea lifted our stern. The plane bounced under the shock, its six guns fired a spraying burst, and its belly tank was jolted into the propeller, which slashed it through and through, and spattered flaming gasoline over the wings and fuselage.

The fire was soon extinguished, and the pilot was only slightly scorched, but the bullets wounded eleven men on the island and damaged five planes on the deck.

Our pilots were briefed this afternoon for tomorrow's strike against Tokyo. The squadron ACIOs announced the positions of the rescue submarines, distributed charts of the target area, and threw photographs of the city on the ready room screens:

"This area here," one of them said, "is the Asakusa district, which has a population of 100,000 to the square mile. It is also a transportation center, as you can see. Fire experts agree that Tokyo's fire defenses are inadequate, and our latest word is that this district is still burning from previous strikes. Experience in Europe has shown that if you bomb something already burning, you scatter the fire.

"The question comes up, 'What about the Imperial Palace?' Well, there's nothing in the Op Plan that forbids an attack on the palace, but it's important to bear three things in mind. First, the Son of Heaven will be below ground. Second, the palace is fireproof. Third, it's certain to be one of

39

the most heavily defended places in the world. Now, has anyone any questions?"

A voice: "Yeah. When are we going home?"

When the ACIO had finished, Fritz Wolfe stepped up: "On the take-off, use a lot of deck. Hold your plane on the deck as long as you can. Then join up on the man in front of you, and as soon as you fill in your section, fill in your division. Don't step down as much as you've been doing; you make it tough for others to get lined up. If we meet opposition before we reach land, we'll take it on right there. But remember this: when you're over water with a low overcast, it's rugged fighting, so stay together! I'll ground any man who breaks formation and goes chasing planes by himself. Further, I'll do my best to stop his awards.

"When we reach land, come back to your rendezvous point every few minutes. We'll get to that target if we can. We're not going to risk our asses to break through the weather, but no handful of enemy planes are going to stop us. When you weave, weave by sections, and stay in there *tight!* If you get sucked behind, you'll get your ass kicked off. OK. I guess that's all."

Some of the boys will carry napalm bombs tomorrow, and they don't like the prospect. They're apprehensive about the kind of revenge the Japs will take if they're shot down. One pilot said, "I'm not worried. I'm an engineer. I'm too valuable for them to torture. They'll put me to work in the Mitsubishi factory."

Another said, "That's fine, chum, just fine! I'll think of you while I'm hanging by my—."

I stepped on something as I was washing up for chow tonight. It was Stew Lindsay's pocketbook, so I took it up to him in flag plot.

He asked, "Where did you find this?"

"In our room, on the floor." The moment it was out, I knew I should have said "on the *deck*," but it was too late then. I looked around to see if anyone had heard my blunder. No one but the Admiral and the Chief of Staff.

I felt like the Reserve officer who figured, last summer, that the war would last two years more. He said it had taken him the first two years to learn to say *deck* for *floor*, *head* for *toilet*, and *bulkhead* for *wall*, so it would probably take him another two to unlearn them. Anyhow, he was starting right then.

February 25th (Sunday). At sea

We'll probably be at our battle stations for several hours, so it was welcome news that came over the loudspeaker at 0900: "Release one man out of every 20 to draw soup. Soup may be obtained at the following places: on the flight deck at Number 3 elevator, on the hangar deck at Number 3 elevator, and at the crew's galley."

Presently one of the signalmen climbed back to flag bridge with a steaming jug. Chaplain Wright joined me in a cup. He'd just been down to see our Jap prisoner, Sadao. The corpsmen in sick bay had made quite a pet of him. They call him "Little Tojo" and they've taught him some English—*coffee, bread, leg, bed,* and so on. When his Marine guard is changed, he says, "Good Marine!" and when one of the chaplains comes in, Sadao folds his hands and bows his head.

After the second strike took off, I went down to air plot to eavesdrop on their progress. The *Yorktown's* call is "Cobra Base," and all our planes have Cobra numbers. As I came in, the radio was saying "One-five-one Cobra, this is 158 Cobra. I am last plane off and have joined up."

One-five-one Cobra acknowledged with "Roger."

A few minutes later we heard a plane on the first strike: "This is 18 Cobra. Air opposition is heavy."

Then 179 Cobra called us: "My transmitter key is stuck. I can not receive. I am returning to base."

Soon another plane was in trouble: "This is 157 Cobra. My oil temperature is up to 100. What do you think of it?"

Someone, probably his section leader, told him, "Return to base."

Air plot warned him, "157 Cobra, this is Cobra Base. Drop your belly tank, put your guns on safe, and expend your rockets!"

"This is 157 Cobra. Wilco! . . . I am unable to expend my rockets."

"Use circuit breaker. I say again, use circuit breaker."

"This is 157 Cobra. I've tried that."

"Try once more. Check your arm-key switch."

"I've tried everything. Is it all right to come aboard?"

Air plot told him, nervously, "Affirmative. Expedite Charlie," and waited. He landed safely.

There are nine Air Combat Intelligence officers aboard:

41

two for the staff; one for each of the four squadrons in the air group—fighter, fighter-bomber, torpedo, and bomber; one for the air group itself, and two for the ship. All intelligence channels through the ships' ACI office, which is only a few steps from air plot, so I looked in to see if Pat Garvan had any news that air plot had missed. Pat passed it to his assistant, Dave Gibson: "How about it, M-36? Got anything hot?"

Dave said, "Not a thing, Q-14."

I asked, "What's all this M-36, Q-14 stuff?"

"We're just being mysterious," Pat explained. "Dave and I signed up for Intelligence because we thought there'd be a lot of wonderful cloak-and-dagger business. There wasn't, so we're supplying our own."

1025: Back in air plot. "Anything new?"

"A Cobra chicken is down. He's only ten miles from a rescue sub, but he's in a mine field. Don't know who he is or whether they can pick him up."

A "chicken" is a fighter plane, a "hawk" is a dive bomber, and a "fish" is a torpecker.

(Later: The sub picked him up.)

1110: On the flight deck. One of our strikes is returning. As each plane lands and taxies forward to be chocked, the pilots tell their story in pantomime. Passing the bridge, they grin and hold up as many fingers as they have shot down enemy planes. (I once saw Alex Vraciu, with a grin like a slice of watermelon, wave six fingers at Admiral Mitscher, on the *Lex.*) Further up the deck stands a radioman, tapping his ear. If the plane's radio was satisfactory, the pilot makes a circle with his thumb and forefinger or holds up his thumb; if it wasn't, he turns his thumb down. Last, when the plane is chocked, the squadron Engineering officer steps forward, holding up an inquisitive thumb. Again the pilot replies by holding up him thumb; or, if anything was wrong, he climbs down and says, for instance, "Crate's OK, but my port inboard gun is jammed."

We must be still expecting an enemy attack, because as soon as this strike is landed, Pappy Harshman orders over the bull horn, "De-arm and de-gas torpedo planes and bombers!"

The crews are happy to obey. If a bomb or a *kamikaze* is going to hit us, there'll be a lot less damage if our planes have empty tanks and bomb bays.

1430: Flag bridge. "Sweep pilots, stand by to start engines! . . . Stand clear of propellers! . . . Start engines!" The fighters' engines spit and roar, except for Number 5 in the front rank and Number 59 in the rear. The crews crank them, then they roar, too.

We are running with the wind and we must turn into it before we can launch. Pennant 2, Pennant Zero, First Repeater, Turn, are two-blocked at the yardarms—"Prepare to come left to a course of 200." All ships in the task group hoist similar signals. Ours is hauled down—"Execute!"—and the whole formation begins to swing, the ships heeling over to starboard.

F6F Number 65 is poised on the port catapult, Number 26 on the starboard. Behind them, Numbers 5, 30 and 43 move into line.

The Fox flag is hoisted at the dip—"Stand by to launch planes!" A green flag is stuck into a socket at Flight control— "Ready to launch." Fox is two-blocked—"Launch!"

Number 65 is thrown into the air, then 26. Another goes, and another. The pilot of the seventh plane waves at me as he moves into position. It is Joe Mayer. When I wave back, he points at the side of the fuselage and shakes his head, grimacing: his plane is Number 13—a number which Joe hates and fears. . . .

2030: Church services in the forward messing compartment are strange enough anyhow, what with rocket racks around the bulkhead, but tonight a file of naked men kept passing behind the "pews." The crew had been at GQ all day, and this was their first chance to take a shower.

February 26th. At sea

Only three of our planes were shot up yesterday, and Joe Mayer's Number 13 was one of them—he took a 20mm shell in his port wing. Joe said, "Hell, I'm not squawking! I expected to get the works and I got off cheap. Ever hear about the *Ommaney Bay?* Out of every five landing crack-ups her air group had, four of 'em were by 13s. One time the *Ranger* had this accident—I don't remember what it was—anyhow, five planes were damaged on the hangar deck, and three of 'em were 13s. The first man killed in Fighting 3 was flying Fox 13. If you think *I'm* nuts, *you're* nuts!"

Some carriers allow crewmen to taxi the planes when the deck is being respotted, but the *Yorktown* requires pilots to do the taxiing, which they consider a nuisance. This afternoon, when Pappy Harshman ordered, "Taxi pilots, man your planes!", they swarmed up from their ready room shouting, "All right, boys! Hit 'em low, hit 'em hard, hit 'em often! Let's go!"

February 27th. At sea

They gave us GQ at 0025, a time when the groundswell of sleep was rolling me like a drowned man. I woke up Stew, who couldn't get his eyes clear enough to tell the hour hand from the minute hand, and kept protesting, "It's 5 o'clock! Routine GQ, routine!"

Flag bridge was empty, under a brilliant moon. The cockpits of the planes below were shrouded, but the white wedges on their tails and starboard wings were almost luminous. Then, with one voice, the *Yorktown* and the ships to port opened fire (I couldn't see what was happening to starboard). I cupped my hand around the mouth of the speaking tube—for fear the blast of our 5-inchers would slam my face against it and knock my teeth out—and poured a sparkling account of the action into flag plot, only to learn later that flag plot had forgotten to uncap its end of the tube.

We ceased fire and waited. A *Randolph* night fighter flashed past us, low, heading west, and presently "Secure from General Quarters!"

Happy birthday to the Admiral, and back to bed at 0125.

Fueling again, this time from the *Tomahawk*. (And Admiral Mitscher's call-sign is "Mohawk," and the *Monssen's* is "Comanche," and we're "under way for Indian Country." Who's running this fleet, Admiral Spruance or Buffalo Bill?) The destroyers that take their turn on her starboard side show signs of the recent weather. The *Hailey's* paint is flaked and peeling all along her hull; so is the *Heerman's*. But we have eyes for only one thing: the mailbags on the *Tomahawk's* deck. I can count more than a hundred of them, and through the glasses I can make out "58.4" on the yellow labels. That's us! The bags come aboard in slings, and presently we hear the bugle gaily singing mail call:

> I got a letter!
> I got a letter!
> Letter, letter,
> Postcard too!

If the Japs were smart, they'd hit us right now. On mail day, there's not a man on the ship who can give more than a quarter of his attention to his job.

February 28th. At sea

But heading back to port. It was an easy, lazy day, so I stopped by Ready 2 for a return match at gin rummy with McLeroy.

"I've just cut a nice slice off Mayer," he said, "but I'm still hungry for red meat. That Mayer—! Did you ever see such a numb-noggin? Him and his 13s! Me, I haven't got a superstition in the world. . . . Well, I guess that's not strictly true. I just naturally hate to fly when I've been winning at cards. I won $350 playing poker last night, and if I was scheduled to fly today, they couldn't pry me off the deck with a crowbar. On the other hand, when I've been losing, I figure the Jap who can hit me or outfly me hasn't been born yet."

It's just as well Mac's not flying tomorrow either. He gave me another pasting.

Two lines overheard during the game:
"When that Zeke got on my tail, boy, I turned *white!*"
"White? I turned Rinso—three shades whiter!"

Captain Combs invited Proff and me to dinner tonight. One of the stories he told us was about the *Langley's* first skipper. A seaman but no flyer, he conceived the idea of spotting her whole complement of planes on the flight deck and running their engines wide open, to see if he could navigate by their power alone. He tried, too, but it didn't work.

March 1st. Entering Ulithi

1220. "All magazine personnel, man your stations!"
I was in my room when I heard it, and I thought I had plenty of time to finish what I was doing before firing practice started. After my first experience, I didn't want to be caught there again; it was like being inside a kettledrum during "The 1812 Overture." So I was loafing along when— BLAM! My ears rang, my eyes watered from the sucked-in smoke, and a cup of Coca-Cola jumped off the desk onto my pants.
1410. Hendy and I leaned on the rail of flag bridge, watching our entry into the lagoon. The day was scalding, and the

glare was stinging. Close by, Jones called off the bearings of the buoys and navigation points: "Able, two-five-six, three-quarters . . . Baker, three-zero-zero, a half. . . ."

Mueck came by and pointed to the signal he had just hoisted: Pennant 4, William, Charlie, King. "Know what that means?"—"Routine calls of commanders may be dispensed with!"

Jones: "Red nun coming up abeam . . . Baker, 019 . . . Baker, 021½, mark . . . Red nun abeam . . ."

Another signal went up to the yardarm: 4th Repeater, Mike, Speed, Pennant 1, Pennant 5: "For general information, my speed is 15 knots."

Jones: "Baker, 030. . . ."

Hendy said, "You should have been with us here the day the midget subs got in. It was plenty feverish! There were contacts all around us, and depth charges going off, and about half way to that sandspit there, this tanker was burning with black smoke. The TBS went crazy."

"Baker, 039½. . . ."

"They were dropping depth charges all day long. About where that third can is, two Jap bodies came to the surface. We sent a small boat over, but one of them sank before we got there."

1428. The bos'n's pipe, and "Secure from General Quarters! Set material Condition Baker!"

As five bells rang, we turned into the wind. To port was a small tanker. To starboard, a Liberty ship was airing bedding. Ahead was a hospital ship, gleaming white. Crates, cartons, and garbage floated past us. It was strange that no gulls were around.

1442. We began to lose way. Men on the flight deck drifted forward and lined the chain at the ramp, waiting for the hook to drop. A stiff breeze shook their uniforms as if we were seeing them through heat waves.

1448½. A long blast on the bugle: we have let go the hook. The jack broke out on its staff, the engines backed, the foam subsided to a slick, and the guns of Number 3 mount leveled.

The Admiral came out and leaned on the rail beside us, smiling. "Nice trip," he said.

"Yes, sir. Very nice."

I collected my cold-weather clothing from under the desk in flag plot and hung it up in my room. Wonder how soon I'll need it again?

March 2nd. Ulithi

This afternoon, the flag Operations officer, Comdr. Andy Jackson, took me under his wing for instruction. It was like being taken under the wing of the Iron Maiden of Nuremberg.

"We'll begin by giving you a little light reading," he said. "Draw the following material and let me know when you've finished it. Got a pencil?—TFI 1 Able, USF 10 Able, the General Signal Book, General Tactical Instructions, the War Diary, and all our Action Reports. That's all for the present."

I drew them and, with the help of four burly yeomen, got them to my room. The books must have been survivors of *Ticonderoga*, because they were charred and still smelled of smoke. One of them fell open at this passage:

"Revised form for reporting AA action by surface ships:
"Notes: a) REPEL ATTACK FIRST—then collect data for this report."

First catch your rabbit. . . .

Our prisoner, "Little Tojo," left us today, disconsolate, for transfer to a civilian internee camp at Saipan or Hawaii. Lately, he hasn't been practicing his English as eagerly as before, Bill Kluss told me. It seems that the Marine guards got to him when the corpsmen weren't around, and taught him a number of hideous obscenities under the guise of conventional greetings. The trick came out when one of the chaplains asked, "How's your leg this morning?" and Little Tojo, with a cheery smile, told him to— .

March 3rd. Ulithi

By now I'm well into my reading assignment. There's nothing like a Navy textbook to give you a picture of the professional Navy mind. Consider this sample from a section entitled "Man Overboard Procedure":

> *511. There are two prescribed procedures for man overboard, the peacetime man overboard procedure and the wartime man overboard procedure.*
>
> *512. The peacetime man overboard procedure will always be used in time of peace. . . .*
>
> *513. The wartime man overboard procedure will be used ONLY IN TIME OF WAR. . . .*

Or this one:

> 189. *STANDARD DISTANCE.—The distance pre-scribed in type Current Tactical Orders . . . between adjacent ships. . . .*
> 190. *DOUBLE DISTANCE.—is twice standard dis-tance.*
> 191. *HALF DISTANCE.—is one half standard dis-tance.*

Lord, Lord! They tell 'em that *b,a,t* spells *bat,* but they don't trust 'em to figure out for themselves what *c,a,t* spells. You get the same patient, painstaking superfluities in the definitions of Standard Speed, Two Thirds Speed, and One Third Speed. Half Speed is not defined. Suppose some task group commander suddenly ordered it? I bet the ships would pile up like a log jam in the Kennebec while the skippers scratched their heads and thumbed through their books.

The Aircraft Maintenance officer, Pat Haley, is the inventor of a hellish contraption which he calls the "Mark XIV Mod 5 Hotfoot." He opens out a paper clip, threads on it a couple of pellets of powder from a starter cartridge, wraps this with cotton which he has rubbed into shoe polish, and bends the wire into the shape of pincers, so that once it is clipped onto the victim's shoe, it can't be shaken off.

Last Sunday, Pat found Chaplain George Wright asleep under a desk in Flight Deck Control and slipped him the business. By the time George had wiped away his tears of agony, Pat was gone, and George spent the next five days grilling suspects. The criminal might never have been discovered if Pat hadn't gone ashore to Mog Mog yesterday and filled up on beer and kidded George about his expression when the hotfoot woke him up.

Today George got the Chief Master-at-Arms and hauled Pat off to the brig, along with Doc Voris, who was implicated too, somehow. But he kept them there only long enough to have their pictures taken.

Movie for everybody tonight, "Hollywood Canteen." One scene showed a pair of Spanish dancers stomping around with a lot of click and clatter. A sailor near me said, "So *that's* who bunks on the deck above me!"

Much the best part of shipboard movies is the remarks of the crew. The *Massachusetts* used to put its movie projector on top of Number 3 turret, which was trained dead at the screen, on the fantail. Our first night back in port, after a month at sea, everybody was hoping for a Betty Grable picture, or a Rita Hayworth. Instead, we were given an idiotic juvenile called "Henry Aldrich, Editor." The film had been running for perhaps five purposeless minutes when a bored voice called, "Number 3 turret—fire!"

From the Plan of the Day: "If the strain of our present operation has given you a 'sour disposition'—give its effects to the Japs—not a shipmate. Guard against the hasty flow of ill-chosen words that not only cheapens you, but causes you to lose the friendship of a shipmate. Don't give the Japs the satisfaction of even giving us a sour disposition—it ain't worth it—besides, he has written enough of his own exaggerated glory. From what the mess cooks tell me—a sour disposition, like sour garbage, should be ground up and thrown overboard."

March 4th (Sunday). Ulithi

Fighting 3 had a party at Mog Mog yesterday. This morning I saw the survivors, notably McLeroy, with a long, raw cut on his knee.

I said, "You going to tell me I ought to see the other fellow?"

"We didn't have any fight," Mac said. "We came awful close to it, though. That goddam Gashouse—know what he did? There was this Gyrene lieutenant, nice looking guy, drinking a paper cup of bourbon and coke, so Gashouse staggers up to him and puts his hand around the Gyrene's hand and squeezes the cup, and the drink squirts all the hell over his nice, clean uniform.

"The Gyrene didn't get sore. He put the empty cup down on the bar—the bar had just closed, by the way—and took hold of Gashouse's collar, nice and quiet, and told him, 'Look. I'm not sore, but I just can't let a guy get away with something like that.' He was about to let him have it on the kisser when I stepped in and smoothed things over. No fight, no trouble, nothing."

"How about that knee?"

"That? Oh, I got that when I took Gashouse outside, and the bastard fell down and pulled me down with him."

"Yeah?"

"Yeah."

Since we're at anchor, George Wright could hold services on the hangar deck this morning, instead of in the forward messing compartment. A verse from the Book of Job jumped at me from the prayer book: "He shall deliver thee in six troubles, yes, in seven there shall no evil touch thee."

I'm counting on that! The Tokyo operation was my fifth, which gives me two bisques for the future.

Scuttlebutt says that Air Group 3 will be detached in a day or so and sent home. So far, it's scuttlebutt and nothing else, but the pilots are already making their plans.

March 5th. Ulithi

The scuttlebutt foundry worked overtime today. Air Group 3 is being relieved at once and sent home. No, it's going to Guam for a month's standby. No, it'll be put aboard the *Lex.* The flag is being shifted to the *Bennington*. No, the *Randolph*. No, we'll stay right here. Far, far into the night. . . .

Carl Carlson and I caught some sun in the portside catwalk this afternoon. He was so convinced that Air Group 3 was homeward bound, he'd already packed his flight gear.

"I don't know why I bothered with it," he said. "I don't expect to do any more flying for one hell of a long time, if ever. I might as well have thrown all that junk away—all except my helmet, of course. I'm going to have that framed."

"Your helmet? Why?"

"On account of my daughter's shoe. Renee Lee. She's two years old, and this was one of her first pair of shoes. I sewed it on the back of my helmet for good luck. Didn't you ever notice it?"

"I don't think so. Did it work?"

"Did it *work?* Listen. Since I started wearing that shoe, I was never shot down, never wounded, never even ground-looped a plane. I never even had an accident of any kind, except for two blown tires. One of them was an old tire on a training plane, and the other was here on the ship. The Landing Signals officer took the blame. He brought me in behind a gun mount, and I had to stand on the left rudder to slip it in. You know Noel, my wingman? He gets a bang out of watching that shoe when I push over. He says he can tell the angle of my dive from the angle the shoe stands out behind.

"I wouldn't any more fly without that shoe than I'd fly without my guns. When I was with VF 301 down in Espiritu

50

last year, I lent my helmet to a friend one day when I wasn't scheduled to fly. After he'd taken off, the skipper told me he wanted me to go up. I told him the hell with it. Not me. Not without my shoe.

"That was the most superstitious squadron I ever saw, 301. Everybody in it carried silver dollars. I've still got mine. I remember one time at Long Beach, it was 5 o'clock in the morning, and I had to buy some gas. The filling station man couldn't change a twenty-dollar bill, so I had to give him my silver dollar. I told him what it meant to me, and he held it for me for four weeks, until I came through there again. The man told me he carried one of them himself."

I asked, "Are those your only superstitions?"

Carl grinned. "Well, when we were flying over Japan, I had a wishbone in my pocket."

"You've got sort of a blanket policy," I said. "Three-way coverage: shoe, dollar, and wishbone."

"Well, the fact is, I've got another one, I guess. See this ring on my right hand? I used to wear it on my left, until one day I was rat-racing in an F4F and I got on my back and got my ring finger jammed between the throttle and the mixture control. The more I struggled, the tighter it jammed. I told myself, 'Now looka-here!' Finally, I took my other hand off the stick and pulled my finger loose, but there were a few seconds there when I thought I was up the creek for sure. Ever since then, I've worn the ring on my right hand. But that's not superstition. That makes good sense." He paused, then added, "Not that the other ones don't, too!"

A new bos'n's mate must have come board since we made port, because there was a voice on the public address system today that I've never heard before. The announcements were made in the usual bos'n's mate's cadence, but the accent was fresh from Brooklyn. The first time I noticed him was this morning, when he announced, "There will be a meeting—of all depottament heads—in the Execcative officer's stateroom —at zero nine o'clock." Navy-fashion, nine o'clock in the morning is written 0900 and spoken "oh-nine-hundred." Nine o'clock at night is 2100 or "twenty-one hundred." You simply don't say, "zero nine o'clock."

"Babe Herman," as we have already come to think of him, threw the ball into the stands again a few minutes later: "The presentation of awards ceremony—scheduled for this after-noon—has been canceled—until ten hunnert—tomorrow morning." Maybe some officer wrote "canceled" instead of "postponed," but I'm sure the Babe threw in "morning" on his own account.

Lank Lancaster, the Assistant Engineer, has his orders and is shoving off for Uncle Sugar. Tonight he came in to show me a farewell present his division had given him—a sheath knife, the finest I've ever seen. One of his machinists had ground a file down so that it had two edges. The tail of the file, now the handle of the knife, had been painted red and fitted with rings of bakelite, plexiglas, and duralumin, smoothed and polished. The knob was also duralumin, machined from a propeller blade.

The immortal Emanuel Pyecroft said of Mr. Hinchcliffe, "He's what is called a first-class engine-room artificer. If you hand 'im a drum of oil an' leave 'im alone, he can coax a stolen bicycle to do typewritin'."

I believe our machinists could equip the bicycle with a built-in chronometer.

March 6th. Ulithi, Guam

This morning, Admiral Mitscher held a press conference on his flagship, the *Bunker Hill*. It was the first time I'd seen him since we were on the *Lex* last year. There was no change; he still looked like a cherubic hickory nut. Seven chevrons still appeared when he wrinkled his forehead, and he still spoke so softly that no one ten feet away could hear a word he said.

One of the correspondents asked him, "Sir, have you any theory why the Japs didn't put up stiffer opposition when we were off Tokyo?"

"Yes," the Admiral said, "I have."

The whole room fell silent. "It's a rather curious theory," he went on, "but I give it to you for what it's worth. I believe that they—" and right here his voice died away completely. He continued to speak for perhaps three minutes, but I don't believe even the men next to him caught a word of it unless they were lip reading; and when he had finished, nobody dared ask him to repeat.

Someone said feebly, "Very interesting. Thank you, sir." And that was that.

This was field day on the *Yorktown*. As the old Navy proverb goes,

Six days shalt thou labor and do all thou art able,

*And on the seventh—holystone the deck and scrape the
cable.*

The whole ship was painted, scrubbed, and shined. She
was already spotless, but today the men chased dirt like a
crew of Old Dutch Cleanser girls. For instance, no matter
where you stand on the vast hangar deck, you're not more
than four feet from an eyebolt, which is used for tying down
planes. There must be thousands of these bolts set in the deck,
yet the men took a compressed-air hose to every single one of
them and blew out the dirt they couldn't reach with their
swabs and brooms.

I was aboard a certain cruiser once and heard a sailor say,
"You could eat your chow off the deck of this ship. The
chow's already so goddam filthy, it wouldn't hurt it none."

In the afternoon, I took a boat in to a Falalap island and
caught a plane up to Guam. It's like a family reunion. Half
the ACIOs I've ever known are here—Frank Bowen, Roger
Weed, Will Player, Smith Bowman, Hank Fonda, Paul Nelson, Peter Lewis, Jim Britt—Lord knows who-all else.

Most of the boys are on CINCPAC's staff, but Frank
Bowen is with the Commander Forward Area, Vice Adm.
John Hoover. I asked Frank if it were true—as fleet rumor
has it—that "Genial John" has never smiled. Not so, Frank
maintained hotly; he *has* smiled, once. Frank wasn't present,
but other members of the staff gave him sworn testimony.
It happened when the Flag Secretary, all excited, burst into
the Admiral's office and, gesturing widely, stuck his fingers
into an electric fan. If you had blinked, you'd have missed it,
they said; but if you'd been alert, you'd have seen Genial
John bare his teeth in a flickering, wolfish grin.

March 7th. Guam

A jeep tour of the island this afternoon, with Frank Bowen.
The Guamanians are the cleanest, gayest, comeliest people
I've ever seen. Many of the girls are as pretty as a little red
wagon. Frank told me he'd heard of one of them, a real
beauty, who had discouraged the Japs by smearing mud on
her face and hair, and never washing once during the whole
occupation.

Near Agana I spied someone I hadn't seen in years—Mac
Bridges, staggering along under the onerous title of Officer
in Charge, Department of Commerce and Industry, Naval

Military Government. Mac loves his job and Guam and the Guamanians, and stories about them bubbled out of him. My favorite concerned the old lady from Yido. The accuracy of our bombing in the "softening up" period before the invasion had impressed her tremendously—so much so that she developed a theory that the bombs were attracted by the scent of taro root. Neighbors, less naive, tried to enlighten her, but the old lady stood firm. "You'll see," she said stoutly. Presently a party of Japs took refuge in a cave behind her house. This was her chance. As soon as night fell, she crept out and smeared the cave mouth with taro, then went home and waited. First thing next morning, a direct hit buried the Japs alive, "and now," Mac said, "Nimitz, MacArthur, and Einstein together couldn't convince her that her theory is wrong."

March 8th. Guam, Ulithi

They turned us out at 0400 for the plane back to Falalap. There, I got aboard a personnel boat making the rounds of the harbor. The only other passenger was a captain who had come to take command of a heavy cruiser. He asked if I could point her out to him.

"No, sir. I know her class, but there are several of them here, and I don't know which one she is. Do you know her number?"

"Yes. It's so-and-so."

"We're all right, then. We can find her."

"What's the number got to do with it? How'll that help?"

I looked at him. I thought he was kidding me, but he seemed perfectly serious. I told him, "The number is painted on her bows and counter."

"Is that so?" he said. "First time I ever knew it!"

He may have been pulling a dead-pan gag, but I'll take my oath he wasn't. He was an Annapolis man—I saw the Nugget on his Knuckle, his class ring—Annapolis captains simply don't kid with Reserve lieutenant commanders.

Scraps: Air Group 3 is gone. Mac left me a dozen bottles of beer, and Joe Mayer left me his flying suit.* I'll miss that pair of bums—and Fritz and Carl and Jake and all the rest of them. Air Group 9, which is relieving 3, will have a tough time beating their record.

*Joe was killed that July. He was flying around the country on a bond tour and spun in at some field in the Midwest.

Coincidence: I was rereading Thurber's "The Funniest Man You Ever Saw." The sour character is named "Joe Mayer."

Gene Tunney paid us a visit this afternoon. Five minutes after he pulled up a chair, he looked as if he'd just been fished out of the water. I don't sweat; I just itch.

The lights in our part of the ship were out when I got back. When they came on again, the electric fan started buzzing. It gave me an eerie feeling before I realized that the fan was on the same circuit. Incidentally, the dial numbers on the ship's telephones are luminous. Not a bad idea.

Something new at the movies tonight: staff officers have been given a row of reserved seats, directly in front of the assistant department heads. Carl Ballinger enraged Pat Patterson by turning around and telling him, "Let me know if you miss any of the picture, sitting way back there, and I'll fill you in later."

March 9th. At sea

We put to sea this morning to exercise the gunnery department and the new air group. Pat Patterson invited me up to his battle station, Air Defense Aft, so I had a box seat for the whole show. The guns had the first workout. As soon as the towplane came within range, the 5-inchers cut loose. Their shells walked up the sky, leaving heavy black footprints, until they overtook the sleeve; and the instant it slowed, indicating a hit, everybody topside cheered. A carrier's guns are strictly defensive weapons, so we all have a vital interest in the efficiency of our gun crews. George Earnshaw and Pat have trained their boys well. They knocked down all five sleeves, three of them with almost the opening salvos.

Every time a sleeve started to fall, one of Pat's talkers shouted, "Sure ragged that one, didn't we, Mr. Patterson?" If a sleeve floats down, writhing, it means a clean hit. If it falls fast, end foremost, it means only a probable hit—a shell fragment has cut the tow wire, maybe well ahead of it. Four of our five hits were clean.

Afterwards, the air group staged a mock attack that was beautiful to behold, but terrifying. One instant, not a plane in the sky. The next, fighters, torpedo planes, and bombers were swarming about the ship like monstrous hornets. You don't see how gun crews as good as ours, even, could possibly keep them off. The torpeckers flipped their big TMBs around as if they were F4Fs. One of the fighters barreled down so fast, he ripped off his starboard horizontal stabilizer; somehow, though, he pulled out of his dive, and sprinted off with the rest of his squadron.

The pilots were smart on attack, but pretty sloppy in the landing circle. Their interval was poor, and most of their approaches were much too high. However, they had only one barrier crash, and that wasn't serious.

March 10th. Ulithi

After supper, Pat Patterson said, "Did I ever show you a pitcher of my bird dog? Handsomest dog you ever did see. Come on 'long to my room, an' I'll show her to you."

He took the picture down from a dozen snapshots pasted on the bulkhead. It showed a black pointer with a white chest, lying on a cushion in front of a cabinet of guns. "Look at her: ain't she pretty? Bet you never saw an all-black pointer before, not countin' that little white tick on her bosom."

I said no, I never had, but I'd seen an all-liver pointer once, named Pepper.

"Bet he was crazier'n hell," Pat said. "Never saw a heavy-livered dog that warn't." He took the snapshot from me and looked at it affectionaely. "She sure is pretty, ain't she? Funny thing: I bought her when I was crazy an' I don't know a thing about her—what her lines are, what I paid for her, how ole she is, nothin'. I just come to, standin' in my house with the dog in the crook of my arm. This was after the horse fell on me out birdshootin' an' broke my back, an' I used to have these crazy spells. But that there spell was a good one—best one I ever had, gettin' a dog like that."

"What's her name, Pat?"

"Gretchen. Funny name for a bitch, ain't it? Funny how she got it, too. There was this old gal of mine, worked in a bank, an' I had to get this note covered, so I called her up an' I said, 'Gretchen, sugar, you jus' take some gol' for me an' put it on top that there note o' mine, an' I be around at three o'clock this afternoon an' everything be all right.'

"She said, 'You know what you askin' me to do, don't you?'

"I said, 'Sure I know what I askin' you to do, an' I gonna make it up to you real soon. Now, don't you worry. You jus' put some gol' on top that note for me till this afternoon.'

"Well, we had us a close call, but everything come out all right, an' I was so much obliged to Gretchen, I began study-in' how I was gonna make it up to her, like I promise. Sure 'nough, when I come to with this pretty little bitch in my arms, hot dog, right away I knew what I was gonna do! I named her Gretchen an' I called up the real Gretchen an' tol' her.

"You know what? Damn if she ever spoke to me again!"

This climate! . . .
From the sheets that never dry out—from the prickly heat that never dries up—from the sourness of my clothes—from the torture of my razor, which leaves my face looking as if I'd massaged it with a nutmeg grater—from cramps—from the shirt that is stuck to my back two minutes after I've put it on—from short tempers—from lassitude—from all this, Good Lord deliver me!

March 11th (Sunday). Ulithi

Over to the *Bunker Hill* for dinner with Bill Connors. Afterwards, we were sitting around his room when the bugle suddenly sounded off. Bill and I kept talking, until we heard the noise of running feet.

"Hold on!" one of us said. "Wasn't that Air Defense?"

It certainly was! We had refused to believe what we had heard. The nearest enemy base, Yap, was 130 miles away, but the Japs had nothing there. Still, Air Defense had blown, so we went topside, grumbling at being turned out for a rehearsal at such a time of night.

The first thing we saw was a pillar of smoke, white in the glare of a searchlight, pouring from an *Essex*-class carrier nearby. Fire was eating at the base of the pillar, and every few seconds the whole stern of the ship shuddered under an explosion, and the fire leaped, and the smoke boiled.

"There she goes!" someone kept yelling. "There she goes!"

Nobody knew which carrier she was, or what had happened to her. Rumors were flitting around like chimney swifts: The victim was the *Hancock,* and a torpedo warhead had exploded; she was the *Essex,* and a *kamikaze* had hit her; she was the *Randolph,* and her magazines had let go; no, an F6F had crashed on her deck. The rumor that alarmed me most was that the whole fleet was getting under way at once. If this turned out to be the McCoy, when would I get back to the *Yorktown?*

By the time the fire was under control, and secured from Air Defense, the facts began to filter through: the ship was the *Randolph;* a *kamikaze* had plunged through the after end

57

of her flight deck; the fleet was not putting to sea; the regular routine of the harbor would resume in an hour or so.

I made the *Yorktown* around midnight and found Stew Lindsay anointing a pair of skinned knees. He had been at the movies, he said, when he saw smoke burst from the *Randolph,* then heard the first explosion. He jumped to his feet for a better view, just as everyone else went flat on the deck, and he was clipped from the rear.

"I don't know who did it," Stew said, "but he's got a wonderful future as a blocking back with the Green Bay Packers."

No one here seems to know any more about the attack than they knew on the *Bunker Hill.* I guess we'll get the straight word tomorrow.

March 12th. Ulithi

Here is an approximation of what happened last night:

There were two *kamikazes,* both of them twin-engine bombers with crews of three, all wearing green and yellow "zoot suits." It's not certain where they came from, but the logical presumption is that they refueled at Yap. One pilot evidently mistook the lights on an island for a ship, because that's where he crashed, injuring fourteen men. The one that hit the *Randolph* killed 25 and wounded 130. Even so, she was lucky. If the attack had come a little earlier or a little later, or if the plane had crashed a little farther forward, casualties would have been far higher. As it was, most of the ship's company was watching a movie, amidships on the hangar deck, and the explosion reached only the very rear of the audience.

The fleet is still pretty jumpy today. We were called to GQ at 1300 and again at 2200. The first one caught me doing sack duty. I threw on my clothes, stuffed a pair of socks in my pocket, and lit a shuck for the bridge. False alarm. The second one blew just as we were putting the beer on ice in Tripp's and Reis's room. Darkness and silence settled over the harbor until the one light left was a welder's torch on a cruiser a few berths away, and the only sound was a harmonica in the 20mm gallery below flag bridge. Another false alarm. When we got back to the room, the beer was cold.

I was trying to locate Hendy this afternoon. He wasn't in his room or in flag office, so I asked the quarterdeck to pass the word for Lieutenant Commander Henderson to dial 658. The bos'n's mate of the watch was Babe Herman again, and this is what he broadcast: "Now will Lieutenant Commander Jenkinson please dial 56—belay that last woid!—please dial 658."

March 13th. Ulithi

Task Force 58 is being reshuffled for the next operation, and they're giving us the luckless old *Intrepid*. As Jesse James put it, "There isn't a man in this task group who's not glad she'll be along. If any ship is going to get it, it's sure to be the 'Dry I.'"

Two more false alarms today: GQ at 0800 and Air Defense in the middle of the movies. The harbor blacked out completely, but the stars were brilliant. The Big Dipper was hanging upside down on our port bow, close enough for you to shatter it with a club. We were pacing flag bridge, waiting for developments, when the TBS suddenly broke the tension: "Hello, Saniflush. This is Fairytale. A whaleboat is adrift 200 yards astern of us. Can you recover it? We have no facilities."

I've begun to think that Limey officer was pretty savvy— the one from the *Victorious* who told me. "If we ever go to war with you, we'll duck battle for the first six months and let you wear yourselves out standing General Quarters."

Tomorrow we sail.

March 14th. At sea

The word was passed at 0555 to "Man special sea and anchor details." I'd finished breakfast, so I went up to the fo'c's'le to watch us get under way. The First Lieutenant, Comdr. John Brady, was standing in the port chains, a small platform overhanging the bow. Whenever he had time, he explained the operation.

"The first thing to do is warm up the anchor engine, connect it to the chain, and remove the stoppers—those things there that hold the chain firm. Then, when we get the word from the pilothouse, we heave in to short stay. At anchor, you know, you have out enough chain to equal four-and-a-half times the depth of the water. We've got 21 fathoms here, so we had out 90 fathoms of chain. Short stay is only one-and-a-half times the depth, or 30 fathoms. We heave in to short stay just before we get under way.

"You'll hear a lot of arguments about when a ship is under

way. Well, she's under way the instant the hook comes free of the bottom, whether the ship is actually moving or not. Remember that! You aviation boys, what you don't know about seamanship—"

He growled awhile, then went on with his explanation. "A chain is measured in 'shots' of 15 fathoms. You've got five fathoms of chain from the hook to the swivel, then comes the first shot. You can tell where you are because three adjacent links are painted white. Same with the second shot: white, red, white. The third shot has got alternate links—"

Just then his talker spoke into his phone, "Aye-aye, sir!" and turned to Commander Brady: "Pilothouse says heave in, sir!"

"Heave in!" Brady shouted.

The anchor engine began to grunt, and the huge links clanked as they snapped into place on the wildcat. Brady pointed to them: "See how clean they are? That's because we've got a coral bottom. If this was a muddy bottom, the last 60 fathoms would be a goddam mass of muck and slime. Now lean over here and look at the chain coming up. Vibrating like a harpstring, isn't it? Watch!"

The engine was running more slowly, grunting more loudly. Suddenly the chain stopped vibrating, and the engine ran faster.

"Anchor's aweigh!" Brady said.

"Anchor's aweigh!" his talker reported.

The bugle blew one long note, the jack was hauled down from its staff, the huge 15-ton hook broke water, and the *Yorktown* followed her mine sweepers and destroyers toward the open sea.

The Chief of Staff has made me an assistant duty officer on this operation. Delighted, I looked up the new watch bill and found I was down for the forenoon watch today. I'd been on duty only a few minutes when I was told to order a change of course from 355 to 010. I shackle-coded the new course, checked the command's call-sign ("Russia"), the task group's ("Quebec"), and those of two ships I would ask to acknowledge receipt, and went on the air by TBS: "Quebec from Russia. Quebec from Russia. Signals, execute to follow—"

Commander Jackson snatched the phone from my hand and shouted into it, glowering at me, "Hello, Quebec-uh! This is Russia—" and completed the order.

Like a dope, I had absently used the old Solomons doctrine, which taught us to say, "Eskimo from Bloodhound," instead of "Hello, Eskimo. This is Bloodhound." My mistake was something less than catastrophic, but it was still a mistake, and I felt like a chump.

When I was relieved at 1145, Jimmy Smith, who had heard the whole business, gave me some comfort. "Never mind," he said. "Remember the day we put into Ulithi? Well, I had the morning watch and the first time I picked up the phone, I ordered a course of 478 degrees and a speed of 64 knots—I was using the day before's shackle code. Not only that, but I asked Scalawag to acknowledge—the *Hailey*, which had been detached and had already shoved off. The Admiral heard it all, too."

After lunch, we turned into the wind to land replacement planes. Out of three that came aboard in a row, an F6F blew out both tires; an SB2C bounced 30 feet in the air, then crashed down all splayed out; and another F6, the last plane in the landing circle, made ten passes before Dick Tripp was able to give it a cut.

The blades of the SB2C's prop bent at right angles when they hit the deck. Frequently they slash right through it, plowing up chunks. On some ships, the men in the ACI office, which is just below the flight deck, never stand up during landing operations. They don't like those wild blades coming into the room with them and whizzing past their scalps.

Flying fish are skittering all around us, although more of a sea is running than they usually like. Off to port, the *St. Louis* is sticking her nose in deep. When she pulls it out again, white water streams from the three guns of her Number 1 turret like spaghetti from the tines of a fork.

March 15th. At sea

A Navy dispatch board is an abridged condensation of a tabloid written in telegraphese. Like any other newspaper, much of it is devoted to routine information, the equivalents of "Arrivals of Buyers" and "Poultry for Sale"—utterly uninteresting to the general reader. But as you leaf through the board, you come upon single dispatches, even single lines and phrases, that are page-1 stories in capsule form. You find comedy and tragedy, pathos and bathos, obsequiousness and impertinence, irony, pomposity, and stupidity. You see the reflections of incisive minds and buttery minds. You read superb prose and gibberish.

61

Here's a sample from today's harvest: OFFICER RECOV-ERED IS ATTEMPTED SUICIDE. Why should an American naval officer try to commit suicide at a time and place like this? Disintegration under past ordeals? Terror of the ordeal to come? Domestic or financial troubles? The destroyer that sent the dispatch gave no details.

Here's another, from Iwo: JAPS CONTINUE TO BOO-BY-TRAP OUR DEAD. And another: BELIEVE MISSING BODIES IN FLOODED COMPARTMENT. And here's the dispatch that followed it: ISSUE OF BLACK PEPPER TO GENERAL MESS SHALL NOT EXCEEED 36 POUNDS PER THOUSAND MEN PER MONTH.

The finest dispatch I ever read was one that Admiral Halsey sent to his task force just before the Battle of Santa Cruz. It said, ATTACK REPEAT ATTACK.

Today's scuttlebutt: After this operation, the *Yorktown* will be exhibited at the Boston Navy Yard.

The Japs are pretty fancy when it comes to naming their ships, especially their destroyers. You get this kind of thing: *Okikumo*, "Distant white clouds"; *Ayanami*, "Waves whose beauty suggests figures woven in silk"; *Oboro*, "Haziness diffusing moonlight"; *Siranui*, "Phosphorescent foam"; and *Tatikaze*, "Wind caused by the stroke of a sword." After such Shelleyan fancies, it's a relief to find that Jap place names are as matter-of-fact as ours. Satamiski is "Sandy Point," O-Shima is "Large Island," Miname Dake is "South Peak," and Nagahama is simply "Long Beach" with cherry blossoms in its hair.

My wrist watch stopped dead today. The mainspring seems to be all right, so I guess I've been standing too close to the big compass magnets.

March 16th. At sea

The best time of day on flag bridge is between dawn and sunrise, right now. The ships in the task group east of us begin to loom darkly against the paling blue horizon. Men stumble out from the island and up from below-decks, yawning and stretching and taking deep breaths of the fresh morning air. I sneaked five minutes' worth, then returned to flag plot's mustiness.

Babe Herman comes on the squawk-box: "Now, Sullivan, bos'n's mate thoid class, foist division, dial zero—belay that woid!" A long pause, then another whistle, and "Sullivan, bos'n's mate *foist* class, *thoid* division, dial 760!"

Fueling day. From a mile astern of our tanker, we can catch her greasy smell. Most tankers are extraordinarily clean. I spent four days on the *Tappahannock*, back in '43, and your nose would never have betrayed her cargo. They say that smell is the strongest stimulus to memory, but if I ever wanted to re-create shipboard life, I'd be hard put to it to find a scent that would summon it. Except for coffee and burnt powder, I don't believe a warship has any characteristic smell.

I could do it by sounds, though. There are a dozen to choose from, any one of which would make the *Yorktown* or the *Lexington* take shape before my mind's eye: the irregular rattle of the shutter on a blinker; the ticking of a 40mm director, and the clamor of the 40s themselves, like a regiment of recruits trying to keep step on an iron stairway; the muffled roar of the blowers; the clank of a tool dropped on a metal deck; the riveting hammer of the water taps; the grinding SLAM! of the catapult; the soft iambic *pop* of the line gun; and the ripple of the barriers going down, exactly like the ripple of reef points as a mainsail comes about.

As for the gong that calls us to General Quarters, if I hear that same tone ten years after the end of the war, I'll automatically grab for a helmet.

Pat Garvan pointed out an item in the Operation Order: "Commanding officers will take such steps as are necessary to insure that pilots are given information only on a single phase at a time." This seems innocent, but its implications are sinister; a captured pilot who knew the plans for the following week, or even the following day, might be tortured into revealing them.

A white stripe 14 inches wide has been painted around the cowling of all our planes, to make their identity unmistakable on the strikes ahead. The F6Fs now look like the old Franklin car, which I once heard a Negro describe as resembling "a heifer wit' he haid cut off."

Speaking of identification, I'm having trouble distinguishing the *Missouri* from the *Wisconsin*. I'd ask Mueck or one of the other signalmen for the clue that I know they have, if I weren't leery of getting some such reply as I got from a chief signalman on the *Massachusetts*. The *Washington* and the *North Carolina* were with us then. One was painted dark gray and the other—I forget which—was camouflaged, but at dusk or when they were upsun, I couldn't tell their silhouettes apart. Chief Hudson received my problem with the expression of a camel shouldering the last straw.

"Why, sir, he said patiently, "the *Washington* is one foot longer than the *Carolina*."

It was also Hudson who, when I asked how he liked flag duty, complained that it was too exhausting—"Every time the Admiral decides to change course. I got to run to the wing of the bridge and hold out my arm for the turn, so the lady drivers on the ships astern won't go bumping into us."

From the Plan of the Day: "Starting today, all personnel will keep sleeves rolled down and shirts buttoned up. Officers will wear medical kits. No sunbathing. No athletics. Place flameproof mattress covers on mattresses. We are getting into bogey country. Remember, it is an all-hands job to keep this a fighting ship. Be alert, and in all emergencies, keep your head!"

March 17th. At sea

Coop Bright began the morning by putting this on the ticker: TODAY IS ST. PATRICK'S DAY. THE BACK OF MY HAND TO JOE MURPHY AND PAT GARVAN. (Joe is ACIO of VBF 9.)

Two letters from Little Tojo came aboard in the last mail. Bill Kluss, who translated them, said that they were written largely in the phonetic symbols which uneducated Japanese employ when they don't know the correct ideographs. One set of these symbols puzzled Bill. Literally, they were *fu-wai-i-ri-n- re-i-ri*. It took him some time to realize that this was the closest Little Tojo could come to "Fighting Lady."

One letter was addressed to Oliver, a pharmacist's mate who had taken special care of him:

"Are you well since I last saw you? When I think of you, I immediately feel like crying. I hope to meet you again soon. I want to go back to the Fighting Lady. And you keep yourself healthy. If this sailor could meet you soon, he would do anything, no matter how painful. You are the one that I liked best of all. I want to work be-

64

cause my leg will soon be healed. I will do that with happiness. I will wait for an answer."

"From Sadao."

The other letter was to the ship at large:

"Recently I was aided in every way possible. No matter how much I could thank you, I do not know if it would be enough. I have wished I could see your faces again. Take good care of yourself. Good-bye and good health.

"From Sadao."

Every day at 1530, unless flight operations are going on, Joe Moody makes a short talk over the PA system, giving us news of the ship, plus whatever dope he has been able to collect from the Admiral, the skipper, and the ACI officer. This afternoon he broke the story that we were heading for Japan again, and soon as his broadcast was finished, Captain Combs took the mike:

"Chaplain Moody has told you of our scheduled strikes for tomorrow. These are to be followed by others which will keep us close to the Japanese coast for several days, while our air group works them over. Enemy attacks can be expected at any time, day or night. You all know how suddenly and effectively they can hit us if our guard is down. The suicide divers strike, as a rule, where we are weakest, or where surprise is effected. Experience indicates that in many instances they turn away from ships throwing up a heavy blanket of accurate fire. We must at all times be ready for them. Our lookouts must be alert to pick up and identify planes. The gunners must be quick to open fire, once the enemy is sighted. We must knock them down if they come at us.

"All hands topside must have their steel helmets and protective clothing immediately available. Your gas masks must be ready for use. Unless your battle station is topside, stay below. There, you are out of the way of the men who have work to do in the exposed places.

"This operation is very important. Its bearing on the future of the war will be great. All the strength we have in ships and planes will be needed as the action progresses. We intend to keep the 'Fighting Lady' in it until the Nips are licked. It's up to us to do everything in our power to protect her. We must be alert for any emergency. That is all."

I was in flag plot during the skipper's broadcast. Almost as he spoke his last words, I heard a familiar *frrrp!* and went out to the bridge to see what had happened. An F6 was being respotted by a handling crew when two of its guns suddenly fired a short burst. The plane's wings were folded, so the guns were pointed downward, and the bullets went through the flight deck. They wounded six men working on a 2C on the hanger deck and one man in sick bay on the third deck. The bullet that hit him penetrated one deck and threaded two hatches, as if it were radar-controlled. Fortunately, none of the wounds was serious.

Nor was the accident that happened a few minutes later. Chief Mueck was passing along the signal bridge when a hoist was hauled down, and the tail of a flag whipped into his face, breaking his glasses. I knew he wasn't hurt; his remarks to the signalmen welled from a limpid heart and an undistracted mind.

Scraps: Flashproof ointment has been issued to all hands. It's a thick, gray cream; nasty looking, but they say it prevents flash burns.

Someone at supper mentioned the accidental firing this afternoon. Pat Patterson grumbled, "That damn Air Department! Minute your back's turned, they shoot at you!"

One of the signalmen pointed out that the *Missouri* is grayish tan, like the *Alaska*, whereas the *Wisconsin* is grayish blue, like the *Alaska's* sister ship, the *Guam*. True, but you can see the distinction only in a strong light, and twilight is the Jap's favorite time of attack.

When I left flag plot at 1600, our course line had staggered another 15/16ths of an inch toward Japan; 4¾ inches to go.

Stew Lindsay has just been promoted to commander, so he gets a room to himself. He moved out today, and Bob Lawrence, the flag Gunnery officer, moved in.

GQ at 2230. Bob Lawrence stumbled out of bed complaining, "Damn those Japs! Why the hell don't they stay home?"

I said, "Look who's talking!"

"I know," Bob said, "but they started it."

The day had been cold, and tonight was bitter. The flight deck was packed with planes waiting for tomorrow's strike. The raw wind jostled them and ruffled the paulins over their canopies, making the lashings slat against their metal skins. We secured after half an hour, but I had hardly hit the sack again when Air Defense rang out, and I beat it back to flag bridge. There was a bright glow on the horizon, far off to port. I called it in to flag plot, but they couldn't explain it;

nobody had reported action on that bearing. A moment later, I saw pale flashes on a bearing of 300°, and I was about to pass the word when I realized that they were exhaust flames from our night-fighter cover. We secured for the second time at 0030. It was still cold and wet, but a few stars were out.

Ralph Delahaye Paine, the publisher of *Fortune*, is a passenger on this operation. The Admiral has given him permission to watch the show from flag bridge, so he kept me company tonight. If the weather is a sample of what we're going to get, I think Del will prefer the wardroom as a vantage point.

From tomorrow's Plan of the Day: "WE STRIKE AGAIN! HEADS UP! KEEP ALERT! USE YOUR HEAD!"

March 18th (Sunday). *At sea*

Does not the boar break cover just when you're lighting a weed? Certainly! And doesn't GQ sound just as you turn on the shower, or sit down to a meal, or start to put in new shoelaces? Certainly! This morning GQ rang at 0457, just as I finished lathering my face. When I reached flag bridge, I learned that our task group had already been in action: an *Enterprise* night fighter had shot down the first bogey of the day at 0104. (Strictly, the night fighter had shot down a *bandit,* not a bogey. A bandit is an enemy plane, whereas a bogey is merely an unidentified plane. However, "bogey" has now been extended to include both terms, just as "shrapnel" has been extended to include bomb fragments.)

Today's targets were four airfields—Tsuiki, Oita, Saeki, and Usa—on the northeast coast of Kyushu. (Somebody says the Japs named the town "Usa" just so they could stamp its manufactures "MADE IN USA.") We were launching our first strikes, at 0517, when a flare was dropped several miles to port. Flares are often a preliminary to a torpedo attack against the ships thus silhouetted. The men on our starboard side strained their eyes into the darkness, but they saw nothing. At 0545, the destroyer *Hailey* reported a glimpse of an enemy plane—too fleeting to take it under fire—but again nothing developed.

Mueck leaned on the bridge rail, his shoulders hunched, as gloomy as a rain crow. "We gonna get it today," he said. "Yes, sir, the old bucket's gonna take one. I saw it in the tea leaves. We gonna get it for sure!"

His predictions were supported by the Combat Information Center (known as CIC, or "Chirst, I'm Confused"); it was calling bogeys all over the sky, and flag plot was relaying the word out to us on the bridge. At 0737, flag plot had just notified us, "Bogey bearing 272, six miles, closing," when flame spurted from the deck of the *Enterprise,* and we could see a plane swerving and weaving through spatters of smoke puffs. We waited for it to fall, but it vanished, still jinking. When we looked back to the *Enterprise,* the fire was out.

(Later: The *Enterprise* took a 600-lb. bomb on her Number 1 elevator. It failed to explode, and she was able to resume flight operations in half an hour.)

The next attack came at 0759. A twin-engine plane appeared out to port, headed straight toward us. A passage from *Moby Dick* suddenly flicked before my mind's eye but vanished before I could grasp it.

Later: It's from the last chapter where the *Pequod's* mates, Starbuck, and Stubb, watch "the down-coming monster" charge their ship:

("The whale, the whale! Up helm, up helm! Oh, all ye sweet powers of air, now hug me close! Let not Starbuck die, if die he must, in a woman's fainting fit! Up helm, I say! . . . Is this the end of all my bursting prayers? all my life-long fidelities? . . . Up helm again! He turns to meet us! Oh, his unappeasable brow drives on towards one, whose duty tells him he cannot depart. My God, stand by me now!")

The plane was directly above the destroyer *Melvin* when our guns opened up. At once both engines burst into flame. The Frances—as I now saw it was—tried to hold its course, but fell off on its port wing and plunged into the sea.

(Later: Fragments of a 5-inch shell hit the *Melvin,* wounding two men. Someone said the battery that shot down the Frances is manned by mess attendants. What we call a "Frances," the Japs call the "Milky Way.")

The *Intrepid's* turn came within five minutes. Another Frances made a run on her and was shot down so close aboard that water splashed over her bridge.

(Later: Bits of this plane killed one man and wounded 13.)

Mueck said, "Now comes up us. We couldn't get hit before the 'Decrepit' got it, but now's when it gets really rugged, and the bastards got all day to pour it on."

I had turned the big signal searchlight inboard and was using its lens as a mirror to patch the gaps in my flashproof ointment when the task group opened fire again. The *Yorktown's* guns were silent, so I could hold my binoculars steady on the plane that was twisting through the shell-bursts overhead. It didn't look like any Jap plane I'd ever seen before.

Its wings were square like a Hamp's, but its tail was square, too. It looked like an F6F. Just then the pilot cocked up his starboard wing in what must have been a desperate hope. The white star was unmistakable.

I was shouting a warning into the tube when a puff appeared directly in front of the plane. It shuddered, then went into a long, reeling glide that carried it across us, out of sight to starboard. There was no use following Jones to the other side of the bridge to see what happened. I knew. Jones came back and confirmed it: "Scratch one Hellcat! I guess you can't blame the boys for being trigger-happy on a day like this."

We secured from GQ at 1048, but Del Paine and I stayed on the bridge, watching the launchings and landings. We drank soup when we could get it, and when the cold became unendurable, we huddled under the lee of the rail, out of the wind, and out of the numbing slip-stream of the planes taking their turns on the starboard catapult.

Del said, "When that Coast Guard cutter was wrecked off Greenland, some of the bodies washed ashore weighed 700 pounds, what with the oil and the ice. They tell me——" GQ again!

Del glanced at his watch. "Twelve fifty-two," he said. "Well, at least we had two hours' recess."

Getting the quick, straight word on the imminence of an attack is pretty important on a tense day. If the nearest bogey is 40 miles away, for instance, you know you have a few minutes' grace before you have to knot up your belly and take your last deep breath. The word reaches flag bridge in two ways. One is through the speaking tube from flag plot, when the flag plot officers happen to remember that you're out there. The other way is by keeping an eye on the gun crews. When they start buckling their chin straps, and pulling their gloves snug, and straightening their visors, you know it's the equivalent of "Get set!"

This time the speaking tube remained silent, but the sudden activity around the guns gave us a warning which Pappy Harshman emphasized: "De-arm all planes on the double, and jettison bombs and rockets!"

Pappy's order couldn't mean but one thing: the Japs had broken through our patrols. There wasn't time to get our waiting planes into the air, out of the way. There wasn't time even to drain their gas and stow their bombs and rockets safely. The Japs were on top of us, and every plane on our flight deck was an individual dump of fuel and ammunition. I found myself humming

Take your last look at the sky and the brook,
And send your last word to the Czar.

The flight-deck crews whisked their little dollies to the open bomb bays, lowered the ugly thousand-pounders, trundled them to the deck edge, and slid them over the side. Other men collected sheaves of 5-inch rockets and dropped them after the bombs. If one of the men—it occurred to me—happened to be named Davis, we might nickname him "Jettison." . . . Del watched the squandering with a taxpayer's eye. About half the planes had been stripped when he asked, "My God! What do those bombs cost—the big ones?"

"Two hundred bucks, two-twenty, it depends——"

Every gun in the task group opened fire at once. Mueck and Jones, who had been on the starboard side of the bridge, came charging around to my side, heads down, shouting something I couldn't hear above the din. They didn't knock me down and run over me—they ran up one side of me and down the other. I saw them duck into the bridge shelter just as a geyser of dirty brown foam spouted higher than our stack, about 75 feet on our port beam. The whole ship seemed to jump clear of the water. The heavy steel hood of the compass leaped off its bracket, and the alidade was flung to the deck. My chin strap must not have been latched, because I remember how my helmet clanged on the deck and how oddly it wobbled.

I made my report over the tube and was trying to remount the alidade when Mueck and Jones sidled back. They waited for the guns to pause, then Mueck said, "Didn't mean to crash you, sir, but when you see us coming, you'll know things are *bad*."

I said, "Tell you what: let's make a couple of rules for this bridge. One, keep the passageway clear, and two, every man for himself. OK?"

"OK," they said. "We got the plane. A Judy. The whole fleet was shooting at it, but it was our guns knocked it down."

The guns came in on cue. They were trained toward the starboard bow, so the rear of the turrets was inboard, and they evacuated their empty brass cases onto the flight deck in a horrible, roaring diarrhea. Presently the ship seemed to shrug herself, and the fire slackened and died. The sour yellow smoke blew away. I heard a faint cheer, and then there was no other sound but the shell cases jingling and tinkling as they rolled with the motion of the deck.

Mueck ran to the starboard side. In a moment he was

back. "Another near miss," he reported. "A hundred feet off the starboard quarter. We got that one too—another Judy. The gun team's really on the ball today."

"I love 'em," Jones said fervently. "I want to kiss every stinking son of a bitch on every stinking gun."

"Me too," Mueck said, "but I'd kiss 'em twice if they'd knock those bastards down *before* they dropped their eggs."

(Later: The concussion of this second bomb put both our gyros out of commission for a short time.)

This afternoon dragged on. Around 1445, one of our strikes began to return. As the second fighter crunched to a stop, two live rockets broke loose from its wings and skidded down the deck. Half the men in the catwalks went flat. The other half watched the rockets in a sort of daze, as if they were too tired to care what happened. The man that picked up one of them stroked its head and patted it before he threw it overboard.

The fifth fighter—it was Number 57—couldn't get his tailhook down. Lee Spaulding had relieved Dick Tripp on the Landing Signals officer's platform, and every time 57 came up the groove, Lee chopped his paddles as a warning. No use; the hook was stuck. The pilot was making his fourth pass when I heard the whine of the turrets training. Somebody yelled "Down!" and we flung ourselves on our bellies.

The deck threw back the thunder of the guns until my head ached, and the swirling smoke made my eyes sting. I didn't feel the bomb hit us. I didn't know we had been hit for a long time after the guns had ceased fire. I was slapping my ears and rubbing my eyes when Mueck came around the forward end of the bridge. The gray battle paint made his face ghastly. He could hardly talk. He gestured over his shoulder and stammered, "Jesus Christ, sir, it looks like a butcher shop!"

"What do you mean? Did we take one? Where?"

"Take one! *Take* one! You should see the mess. This guy's legs, and the blood, and—Jesus Christ Almighty!" He stumbled away, shaking his head and muttering, "I knew we'd get it today! I knew it! I told 'em!"

I couldn't leave my station for half an hour. When I was finally able to cross to the starboard side of the bridge, one of the signalmen told me that the Jap plane—it was still another Judy—had dived out of the clouds straight ahead of us, and had released so low that the bomb was traveling almost horizontally when it struck.

Its course was plain to follow. The first point of contact

71

was the brass rim on the port of the Admiral's sea cabin, sheared smooth. From there it went on to demolish a squawk-box on the bulkhead, clip two small pipes, and cut a two-foot section out of the huge incinerator vent. Next it ripped through the bridge deck and the rail of the 20mm gun gallery, just below and aft. Here it tore both legs off the man on the forward gun and left him hanging in his harness; he died in the middle of a scream. His blood still clotted his gun, and the hole in the deck was rimmed with blood.

The bomb had traveled another 50 feet aft and had dropped to the level of the hangar deck before it exploded. The blast blew two raw holes in the ship's side—one about 13—riddled all bulkheads in the vicinity, silenced Number 5 mount, and started a fire in Number 7. The worst casualties were in a 40mm mount on the hangar deck; three men killed outright, and many more wounded. (Note for Joe Mayer: It was mount Number 13.)

Most of this I learned later. At the time, I could only glance at the damage before I had to return to the port side of the bridge. The sky was still full of bogeys, and the ships were still firing intermittently. Someone told me that we had shot down the plane that had bombed us, and had recovered the pilot, along with a code book.

Jones said, "If anybody shot him down, you can be goddam sure it was us! Those big bastards over there"—he nodded toward the battleships and battle cruisers around us—"they couldn't hit a bull in the ass with a banjo, and I bet by God they claim it was them that did it all! You watch what I tell you!"

The other signalmen crowded around, agreeing loudly. They were talking away their nerves, using the big ships as scapegoats, and they had worked themselves into a fine, noisy rage when Red suddenly pointed and shouted, "Bogey diving!"

I don't know why I didn't hit the deck with the rest. I must have been numb. I stood there in a sort of stupor, peering up at the sky, until I spotted the bogey. It took me a couple of breaths, if I was breathing at all, before I understood why nobody had opened fire, and a couple more breaths before I could trust my voice.

"That's no bogey," I said. "Look at it. It's a bird."

The men got to their feet sheepishly, cursing Red. One of them told him, "Now I know where I seen you before, you blind bastard! You umpired a game between the Nats and the Yanks, and what your thievin' decisions cost me——!"

The sun set in a soft haze of gray and gold, so serene that

my recollection of the day faded with the fading light. But not Mueck's. He continued to mutter, "I told 'em, early this morning. I told 'em we'd take one. I knew it. I'm never wrong."

I asked him, "How about tomorrow. Or can't you tell without your tea leaves?"

"Tomorrow? Hell, tomorrow'll be easy," he said. "That is, if we live through tonight's torpedo attack. . . ."

Darkness fell, and still we stayed at our battle stations. By 2100, though, the radar screen had cleared, and at 2118 we secured. All the way down to my room, I debated whether to eat first, or to take a hot shower and then eat. I was so tired, I couldn't make even this trivial choice; I had to let a coin decide it. The shower was wonderful. The flashproof paint washed away, and my stiff face felt as if it belonged to me again. The chill melted out of my bones. But what if GQ sounded right now, and I had to expose my steaming carcass to that icy bridge? Pneumonia! Whining and shivering, I turned the hot water off, the cold water on. . . .

Coop Bright and I came into the wardroom together. He hadn't time to wipe off his gray paint, and Carl Ballinger greeted him with, "Hey, Skinhead, where've you been all day—taking it easy? First time I ever saw you with any color in your cheeks!"

Pat Patterson was the only one at our end of the table who didn't laugh. His roommate, Fred Weatherford, had been killed by the bomb.

Supper was one of the best. It began with roast chicken and cranberry sauce, and went on from there. I was finishing my chocolate ice cream when the bugle blew Air Defense. The time was 2227. As I reached the bridge, I saw two lights, a red one and a brilliant white one, swooping down the sky toward us. I called flag plot: "Enemy plane trying to crash the ship!"

Even as I said it, I was wrong. "Correction!" I called. "It's a night fighter from the *Enterprise!*"

Too late. I had passed the crooked word. I was so ashamed of myself, I didn't stop by flag plot when we secured at 2315; I went straight below, squeezing a drop of comfort from the fact that I hadn't hounded Red when he mistook the bird for a bogey.

Into the sack at 2330, after seventeen hours on the bridge. Tomorrow I have the morning watch, which means I don't have to turn out until 0330, Japs permitting.

(Later: I asked Pappy Harshman what had happened to Fox 57, who had been trying to get his tail-hook down when the bomb hit. Pappy said, "We told him to land in the water. A can picked him up."

(The part of the account that follows I didn't learn for several days, but this is where it belongs.)

The bomb burst directly below Joe Moody's battle station—Repair 3, a small shop at the after end of the island. As soon as Joe heard the explosion, he dashed out onto the flight deck. A Marine in the 20mm gallery around the corner was rubbing his bloody eyes and screaming. Next to him, another Marine was trying to stanch a jet of blood from his leg. Joe grabbed a stretcher, commandeered three corpsmen, and rushed the blind man toward Battle Dressing 1, at the forward end of the island. On the way, they passed a sailor who pointed to the clipping room and shouted, "Bad ones up there, Father! A lot of 'em!"

Joe told the corpsmen to keep going, and ran up the ladder to the clipping room. Six men were lying on the deck, two with both legs gone. He leaned over the nearer one and asked, "What's your religion, son?"

The man opened his eyes and whispered, "Jewish." He closed his eyes immediately.

Joe lifted him onto a stretcher and helped carry him down to the dressing station. Dr. Bond was bandaging a burnt arm. Joe said, "Here's a bad case for you." The doctor didn't need but one glance. "He's gone," he said. "Put him aside."

As Joe started back up the ladder, a stretcher came down with the other legless man. Joe asked him, "What's your religion, son?"

"Protestant."

George Wright was working in the dressing station, so Joe patted the man's shoulder and told him, "Your chaplain's right ahead, son. Keep your chin up!"

Two of the four men left in the clipping room were desperately wounded. Both were Catholics. He anointed them (he carries the materials for the Last Sacrament in his first-aid kit) and put them into stretchers and helped get them to the dressing station. The other two casualties were able to walk.

By now, the dressing station was overcrowded. Dr. Bond told the chaplains, "We've got to get some of these boys to sick bay. Can you do it?"

Although the ship was still at General Quarters, Pappy Harshman gave Joe permission to use Number 3 elevator. Meanwhile, George Wright was rounding up stretcher-bearers. Dr. Bond could spare only two corpsmen, and most of the men who would have lent them a hand were too busy fighting the fire around the after turrets. George finally mustered two volunteers, and the six of them set to work. Twelve stretchers: they would have to make four trips.

When they stepped off the elevator at the hangar deck, they found the automatic sprinkler in full blast. They sheltered the stretchers as best they could and started forward to the fo'c'sle, where there was an open hatch. The deck was packed with planes. The bearers had to crawl, one dragging each stretcher, another shoving it, to clear the wings and the wheels. It took them five minutes to reach the hatch and ten more to make their way down the ladders and aft to sick bay, undogging each of the watertight doors and dogging it behind them. On their last trip, the water on the hangar deck was ankle-deep.

One of the legless men was being given plasma when they came to pick him up, and there was nobody to hold the flask.

"Hand it to me," the man said. "I'll hold it!"

He held it firmly until it was empty, but he died next morning.

The eighteen casualties were distributed through four rooms. The chaplains stayed with them all evening, passing around cigarettes and water and blankets, helping the doctors and corpsmen, and saying prayers and taking down last messages when the rattle of the ammunition hoist permitted.

Among the worst wounded was a radar technician. Both his arms were broken, and his body was riddled with bomb fragments. The flashproof ointment on his face was caked with blood and smeared with smoke. Joe asked him, "Want a beauty treatment?"

The man grinned, "Sure!"

Joe began to wash him down. Presently the man asked, "Father, what are you spending so much time with me for?"

Joe asked, "Are you a Catholic?"

"Not too good a one."

"Well," Joe said, "we won't worry about that now."

A little later the man said, "I'll tell you a funny thing, Father: I'm glad this happened to me. I'm completely at peace with God for the first time in my life."

Shortly after midnight he repeated it: "I'm glad this happened to me. It's made it easy for me to do what I've been wanting to do for a long time—be part of the church."

Those were his last words. He died at 0200. We lost a total of five men.

The official report on the bombing listed the casualties and ended, "Storerooms B 425-A and B 436-A take water as the ship rolls, but our operating ability is not impaired."

It made me think of a stanza from a Scottish ballad I once read:

> "Fight on, my men!" Sir Andrew said.
> "A little I'm hurt but not yet slain.
> "I'll but lie down and bleed awhile,
> "And then rise up and fight again."

March 19th. At sea

Flag plot was quiet, almost drowsy, when I relieved the watch at 0345. Two or three minutes would pass without a word, without even a sound except the rhythmic, twanging buzz of the TBS. But as the night wore on, and bogeys began to dot the radar screen, the silences became shorter. More and more frequently the CIC talker would announce, "Raid Two, 237, 42 miles, closing . . . 239, 40 . . . 240, 37. . . . Raid Three, 223, 51 . . . 227, 47. . . . Raid Two orbiting. . . . Raid Four, 228, 43. . . . Raid Two opening . . ."

He plotted every new position on his plexiglas dial, making a little *x* with a red grease-pencil, jotting down the time, and joining the *x*'s to show the course.

The tension built up until I felt as if we were being stretched on a mass rack. It was hardest on the officers and men who had nothing to do, who were simply standing by, waiting to be called on. One's collar was dark with sweat; another twirled a key ring around his forefinger, twice clockwise, twice counter-clockwise; a third drew his initials on a message blank, elaborating the letters, shading them, adding scrolls and curlicues.

The CIC talker droned on: Raid Five, 248, 51 . . . Raid Four, 266, 34, closing . . . Raid Five, 244, 47 . . . 244, 43 . . . 243, 38 . . ."

At 0505, the pilothouse reported that flares were being dropped to starboard. We looked toward the starboard ports, knowing that they were closed, but half-expecting them to open momentarily and give us a view. The tension mounted. It was a relief when the Admiral ordered a change in course or speed, so I could distract myself with the mechanics of coding it and putting it on the TBS: "Hello, Quebec. This is Russia. Signals, execute to follow, turn shackle Mike Charlie Baker unshackle. I say again, turn shackle Mike Charlie Baker unshackle. Armada and Gimlet acknowledge. Over."

The *Missouri's* acknowledgment was crisp: "Hello, Russia. This is Armada. Wilco. Out."

The *Frank's* was cheery: 'Hello, Russia! This is Gimlet! *Wil*-co! Out!"

Then the squawk-box spoke: "Flag plot, this is the pilothouse. We understand you want us to come right to course 080."

I tripped the pilothouse key: "This is flag plot. That is correct."

Then I picked up the TBS phone again: "Hello, Quebec. This is Russia. Stand by. . . . Execute!"

The deck tilted as the big ship heeled to port. Pencils rolled across the chart table. The message boards swayed on their hooks, then steadied as we steadied on our new course.

"Raid Six, 241, 59 . . . 240, 57. . . . Raid Five, 238, 24 . . . 237, 22 . . . 237, 19 . . ."

The pilothouse called back at 0600: "Flares being dropped to port!"

"This is flag plot. Roger."

The cigarette smoke grew thicker. It eddied behind you when you crossed the room; it seemed to have substance, to drag at you, as if you were walking through quicksand.

At 0650, there was a whistle and the announcement, "Sunrise! Light ship!"

Jones went to the bridge and took down the light-baffles on the ports. Daybreak seamed our gray faces, but the morning air blew over us gently, and some of the mustiness cleared. Our respite was brief. Jones closed the heavy steel battle ports, which left only half-inch slits of the horizon. The smoke thickened again, and the CIC talker continued, "Raid Six, 277, 23 . . . 279, 19. . . . Raid Six has been tallyho'd. . . . Raid Five, 265, 22, orbiting. . . ."

I watched the clock crawl: 0715, 0718, 0719. The first strike began to take off, against the Kure Naval Depot. I was relieved at 0745, and went out to see the launching. The bridge was cold, so I came back into flag plot for a jacket and was fumbling for it under a desk when the talker cried, *"Enterprise* has opened fire! A bogey is diving on the formation from 260! Alert! Alert!"

You're trapped, here in the flag plot, and you know it. You can't see anything, you can't hear anything, you can't do anything, except try to keep your terror under cover. You grip the back of a chair, or put your hands into your pockets, under your armpits—anywhere, to damp their trembling. You swallow, to wet your throat, so that if someone asks you a question,

77

your answer won't come out in a squeak. You stiffen your neck against your head's attempt to cower down between your shoulders. You jump aboard the first train of thought that runs through your mind, to escape your imagination's conjury—the blast, the crumpled bulkheads, the pinioned leg, and the flames.

The talker spoke: "Bogey is an F4U." Almost at once he clamped his phones tighter to his ears and said, "What's that Bogey 216, 17 miles?"

Seventeen miles is breathing distance, but suddenly there was a confused shout from the bridge, and the noise of frantic feet, and a heavy *slam!* A battle port had fallen, banging the bulkhead. That was all, but from the way I jumped, I knew I needed fresh air. I had started for the bridge when I heard the talker ask, *"Who's* been hit? Who? . . . Dixie?" He turned to the Admiral: "Dixie's just been hit, sir."

Near the PPI scope hung a large cardboard placard, showing the call signs of all the ships and commands in Task Force 58. "Dixie" was the carrier *Franklin*. I picked up my glasses and went out to the bridge. The *Franklin's* task group, 58.2, was twelve or fifteen miles on our port quarter, but the glasses brought it close aboard. I saw an *Essex*-class carrier dead in the water, with a tremendous plume of black smoke rising from her deck. Every few seconds there was a gush of fire, and the whole ship quaked. I counted nine explosions before she fell astern, hull down over the horizon.

Jones said, "That's all, brother! We can tell 'Big Ben' goodbye." He began to polish the lens of his long glass with a piece of tissue. After a moment he said, "This'll be a different ship when the word gets around."

"What word?"

"About losing the 'Big Ben.' She's got Air Group 5 aboard, and we used to have 'em."

Mueck had joined us. "That's right, sir. There ain't a man on the *Yorktown* who didn't have a friend on the 'Big Ben.' "

For the first time, it occurred to me that I had friends aboard her. I looked back at the boiling column of smoke, and I was grateful when Mueck asked, "Remember those rules we made for our bridge club yesterday?—about keeping this passageway clear? Well, I've got a theme song for us: 'Don't Fence Me In!' Pretty good, hey?"

"All I want is the first line," Jones said. " 'Land, give me land.' "

I said, "I've got a song, too. I got to thinking about how we took care of those battleships yesterday, and here's what I made up:

"Wisconsin, Missouri, Alaska, *and* Guam.
Sleep tight! The Yorktown *will keep you from harm.*"

Mueck said, "That's a dilly! That's four-oh! Wait till I tell that one in the chiefs' mess tonight! How does it go again?"

Astern, the black smoke rose higher and higher. (Note for Joe Mayer: *The Franklin's* number is CV 13. Do you wish you were in Dixie?)

0900. The *Enterprise* shoved off, escorted by four destroyers and the light cruiser *Flint*. She is going back for repairs, although she shows no sign of the hit she took yesterday. TF 58 has lost two CV's in two days. If the Japs continue to whittle us down at this rate, it won't be long.

1240. GQ again. (I haven't any recollection of our securing from the first one.) The gong rang just as I finished telling the flag bridge men that I was reading the tea leaves today, and we had drawn a definite bye. I got my helmet on in time to hear this over the speaking tube: "Bogey closing from 200." I sighted along the alidade: 200° was dead into the sun. Worse, the flight deck was being respotted, and the roar of the engines would drown the sound of a diving plane. The task group to port opened fire. Its shells were bursting close to the water, so it was probably fighting off a torpedo attack. I waited for our own guns, my ears clenched against their blast. (That's something else I don't like about this speaking tube duty: you can't put cotton in your ears.) Half an hour crawled by. My legs and back were itching from prickly heat, yet my wrists were cracked with cold. It made me think of New Guinea, which is said to be the only place in the world where you can stand in mud up to your knees and have dust blow into your eyes. I was doped off, remembering the malaria at Milne Bay and the snakes at Dobadura, when they announced, "Secure from General Quarters."

1730. Most of the afternoon, we picked our way through drifting mines. I must have seen twenty of them or more. Mueck and Jones were appropriately caustic when the *Missouri* fired at one and missed, and dropped smoke floats to mark it. The *Independence* pulled wide, leaving it to the *Wisconsin*, who merely dropped another marker. Finally a destroyer came across and opened up on it with her 20 mms. She was still vainly trying to explode it when we changed course to starboard, and the island blotted her out.

Jones shook his head. "If it wasn't for *our* gunners—Jesus! How did that rhyme of yours go again, sir?"

The Plan of the Day ended,

OUR HONORED DEAD

We pray to God their loved ones will understand the real sacrifice they have made. Their loss to us is beyond the expression of words. They shall always be a part of each one of us and this ship we call "The Fighting Lady."
WEATHERFORD, Fred G., Lieut. U.S.N.
JEKEL, Elmer (n) S1c, U.S.N.R., V-2 Div.
BARNETTE, Powell M., S1c, U.S.N.R., 4 Div.
SHERMAN, Edward (n), ART2c, U.S.N.R., Air Group Nine
LUECK, Robert Lee, ART2c, U.S.N.R. Air Group Nine.

March 20th. At sea

Asleep at 2230 last night, up at 0700 this morning for a quick breakfast (we eat later on fueling days), and then back to sleep until GQ sounded at 1055. Twelve blessed hours of it! George Bond's slogan is the one for me: "Back the attack from the sack!" I was so refreshed, I ran the bed-to-bridge obstacle course in record time and crossed the finish line without a wheeze.

Jones had the straight word: "The CAP is chasing a couple of bogeys way the hell and gone out there somewheres. Nothing else on the screen. Everything's copasetic."

We secured at 1115, and I went below for a leisurely shave and shampoo and scrub. These tight woolen hoods we've been wearing under our helmets have given me another area to scratch. Wonder if the tailor shop could run me up a sandpaper suit and cap?

1400. The task group half-masted its colors for the burial of our bomb casualties. The ship's company and the staff, all except the men on duty, fell in on the flight deck, facing the port side. Slowly, rumbling, Number 2 elevator rose into view, bearing the five bodies, each covered with a flag. Joe Moody and George Wright read the service. The words of the Committal were muffled by the wind, but it lulled to let one phrase toll clearly: ". . . the sea shall give up her dead. . . ." The band played "Onward, Christian Soldiers," the Marines fired three volleys, and the elevator sank back to the hangar deck. There, the bodies were lifted to a trestle and tilted into the sea. After the fifth splash, colors were two-blocked, and the word was passed, "Carry on!"

GQ sounded again at 1515, but again it was a false alarm. I was having a cup of hot chocolate in the wardroom, and fondling the idea of a nap, when GQ sounded for the third time. By now the afternoon was perfect: the wind had died, the sun was brilliant, and except for a few small scraps of gauzy cloud, the weather was CAVU, as aerologists describe it—Ceiling And Visibility Unlimited. The line of the horizon was drawn so clearly, the sea and the sky resembled an infinite Afirm flag. From twenty miles away, not only could you pick out the the different classes of ships in the other task groups—the *Sommers* and *Fletcher* destroyers, the *Cleveland* light crusiers, the *San Francisco* heavies—you could even distinguish the *St. Louis* as an individual. In our own group, every rivethead seemed to stand out like a bull's-eye. When the destroyer *Hazelwood* sped past us, vivid in her zebra camouflage, the sparkling air made the red bracket on the port side of her bridge glow as if it were illuminated.

Mueck said sourly, "Yeah, but it works both ways: the clearer we can see our ships, the clearer the Japs can see 'em. They've already hit the 'Big E' again, from what I hear, and they're still after the *Franklin*. Know what we are? We're not cannon fodder; we're bogey bait." ("Pogey bait" is Navy slang for candy.)

Admiral Mitscher has ordered all ships to deliver their photographs and other news material to him by 1800 today. When I stowed my gear in flag plot after we secured from GQ, Commander Jackson was grumbling about it: "Why should I have to detach a can I can't spare, just so some Joe Blow can see his picture in his home-town paper two days earlier?"

I started to tell him why, in twenty-five or thirty well-chosen reasons, but I kept my trap shut (for once). The Annapolis attitude toward the press is suicidal, but can you get them to realize it? Certainly not! In one breath, some of them will refuse to give a correspondent the meagerest dole of information, and in the next, they'll complain that "the goddam Army" is getting all the credit for winning the war.

Well, as Mr. Stubb of the *Pequod* remarked, "Think not is

my eleventh commandment; and sleep when you can, is my twelfth."

2100. As usual, GQ caught me in bed. The night was as beautiful as the afternoon had promised—too beautiful, because the cloudless sky was lit by half a moon which wouldn't set until 0100. I reported flashes of gunfire on the horizon to port, and flag plot told me that one bogey had already been shot down, but several were still on the screen. The task group off to starboard began to fire heavily. Four flares bloomed in the sky to port, and suddenly the *Missouri* loosed four thunderclaps. When a nearby ship opens fire at night, the muzzle flash warns you to brace yourself for the *slam!*, but the 'Mighty Mo' was using flashless powder, and I jumped like a stung mule. One of her shells burst blackly in the very face of the moon. In the silence that followed, I heard George Earnshaw's voice from Air Defense Forward: "Sure as hell, they'll claim another plane shot down!" A moment later the destroyer *McGowan* fired once, twice, and then we secured.

Four GQs so far today, but they add up to only two hours.

Early this morning, an *Independence* ASP strafed a Jap picket boat and left it burning. The destroyer *Heerman* was sent over to see what she could find, and picked seven survivors off a raft, five of them wounded. Two she handed over to Admiral Spruance, two others to Admiral Mitscher, and the last three to us.

Del Paine, who was with me on the bridge tonight, told me he'd gone down to the fantail to watch the prisoners come aboard. The first one's stretcher was halfway across, he said, when our AA batteries opened up. (This was at 1643, during the third GQ.) The *Heerman* was in a dangerous position, tucked under our counter with her own batteries masked; but instead of dashing for open water, she stood by until the poor devil's stretcher was safely across. Not until then did she cast off her lines and move out.

Del said, "If it had been the other way around—if the Japs had been transferring an American prisoner—do you think they'd have been that considerate?"

March 21st. At sea

1015. The CIC talker was relaying an account of a pursuit somewhere north of us: "Bogey 359, 54 . . . 000, 57 . . . the CAP is closing. . . ." Flag plot was like a men's club when a college football game is being broadcast, and the alumni around the radio are smoking and chatting their way through a dull stretch. The Admiral was bent over a chart, the Chief of Staff was thumbing dispatches, Hendy was pouring a cup of coffee.

The talker announced, "The plots have merged. . . ." All conversation stopped. The Admiral looked up intent. Then, "Tallyho! . . ." We leaned forward, watching the talker's lips, as if we could read his next words before we could hear them. In a moment they came: "Splash two Betties!"

"Fine!" said the Admiral.

Commander Jackson said, "Hot damn!"

"I *like* that," Jones said.

Everybody grinned. The morning routine resumed.

(Later: The planes that shot down these Betties belong to the *Wasp*. Admiral Mitscher sent the commander of her task group a wry dispatch: CONGRATULATIONS. I WAS BEGINNING TO THINK IT WAS A LOST ART.)

The sea was so blue today, the wakes looked like Grade-D milk. That's what I miss the worst: fresh milk. I was thinking how I'd settle for a glass of Grade D, even, when the gong clanged and we were called to General Quarters.

Mueck came up with a tube of battle paint: "They've passed the word for all hands to put this on, sir."

Jones said, "Yeah. Two large groups of bogeys coming in. Large ones," he repeated. "We're launching an extra CAP."

When the planes had taken off, the three of us rested our arms on the rail and watched them out of sight. I'd bet we were all thinking the same things: "Two large groups" might mean a hundred planes or more. We'd need every fighter and every gun in the task force to handle them. One of our task groups was scratched; it was far south of us, fueling. Another group was crippled by the withdrawal of the *Franklin* and her escorts. Our own group had lost the *Enterprise*, with a cruiser and four destroyers. The *Yorktown* was a lucky ship, sure, but her luck couldn't last forever, especially with gun crews as tired as ours were. When they're tired, they slow up; they can't help it. A lot, a hell of a lot, was going to depend on those fighter pilots we'd just seen roaring down the deck. . . .

I don't know what made us so pessimistic. It wasn't our normal attitude. We could usually find a laugh somewhere, and there was usually a lot of bravado about "Bring 'em on!" But Mueck and Jones were unnaturally quiet. Wolfe looked more than ever like a lugubrious bloodhound. Even Buck, the most carefree of all the signalmen, paced up and down without shadow-boxing or doing a tap step.

Flag plot's silence thickened our gloom. I called into the speaking tube, "Flag plot——"

A sepulchral voice whispered, "Flag plot, aye-aye."

"This is flag bridge port. Any word?"

"Nothing yet."

"Keep us posted, will you?"

"Wilco."

I asked Buck, "What time is it? How long since we launched that CAP? We ought to be hearing something soon."

Buck pulled up the cuff of his windbreaker. "It's exactly—exactly fourteen-twelve."

A squeak came from the tube: "Flag bridge——"

I rushed to answer: "Flag bridge, aye-aye!" The signalmen crowded around me.

"Flag bridge, CIC has just reported that our fighters intercepted the raid and shot down 14 Betties and four fighters, and the rest have beat it."

The whole bridge burst into a babble of "Yea-a-a-a-ay! What did I tell you? Them goddam Japs, that'll teach 'em! Two bits says Fighting 9 got most of 'em! Boyoboyoboy! What did I tell you?"

Mueck said, "What did *you* tell us? You didn't tell us a goddam thing, bud! You didn't need to tell us. Your goddam teeth were chattering like a goddam dicebox. Your teeth told us plenty, but *you* didn't tell us a goddam thing!"

Our hours are pretty irregular, and we're a little short on sleep, and it's been a good while since we've had any fresh fruit or vegetables, but I doubt if this is enough to explain the appearance of three boils on the inside of my left leg tonight. I know nothing about the physiology of fear, but my guess is that fear can concentrate the poisons in your body—hence my boils.

March 22nd. At sea

Another fueling day, which means we've pulled out of the battle area, which means raids are unlikely, which means we can relax. On the average, we fuel every fourth day. If it were every other day, I'd be the last man aboard to complain.

The flag officers' TBS techniques are as different as their handwritings. Captain Trapnell speaks softly, gently. Jim

Smith speaks crisply, biting off the ends of his words. Stew Lindsay speaks deliberately, as though to a foreigner or to a stupid child. Commander Jackson sticks in a lot of *uhs:* "Hello, Mohawk-uh. Negative-uh." Brod, the flag lieutenant, shouts so loud he hardly needs the phone at all. He reminds me of the only funny remark I ever heard attributed to Admiral King. Some other admiral started screaming in the next office, and King asked his aide, "What's going on in there?"

"He's talking to New York, sir."

King said, "Tell him to use a phone."

The Navy may not love COMINCH, but it certainly respects him. He never steps out of character. I can't remember who told me the story about his going aboard the Presidential yacht for dinner one night. Anyhow, he was carrying a parcel and when he reached the quarterdeck, he handed it to a sailor with, "Son, keep this for me till I go ashore."

The eager youngster said, "Aye-aye, sir!" then added, "Your wish is my command, Admiral!"

King pelted him with those two pieces of gravel he uses for eyes: "You're goddam right it is!"

One of today's dispatches ordered us to remove the white paint from the cowlings of our planes. Good! That collar really fouled up the lines of the F6. For my money, it's the cleanest, most graceful plane in either service. The Liberator is beautiful when it's air-borne, where you can see that slender wing, but on the ground it looks like somebody who had stumbled with a kitchen door on his shoulders. The F6 is a honey wherever you see it, and I'm glad they're taking it out of fancy dress.

Scraps: This afternoon, Joe Moody began his broadcast, "Yesterday was the first day of spring. Today, S-plus-1, a young man's fancy lightly turns to thoughts of striking Okinawa Jima tomorrow." Pat Garvan was outraged: "What does he mean, 'S-plus-1'? Today is SP-plus-5! It's the fifth day after St. Patrick's, isn't it?"

Add to boils and the crud: the poor little lambie's face is chapped so bad, he can't shave.

From the Plan of the Day: "Now we start on one of the most important phases of our present operations at sea—taking the NANSEI-SHOTO Islands. With these in our hands, we will be able to control all the sea-lanes across the Japanese Ill-Gotten Empire. WE STRIKE AGAIN TODAY. GIVE

'EM HELL! HEADS UP! KEEP ALERT! USE YOUR HEAD!"

March 23rd. At sea

The principal actions today took place in early morning darkness, so we couldn't see them, but here's the official account, as written up in COMCARDIV 6's War Diary:

"At 0100, the HAGGARD re-established the contact she had just lost, and dropped a full pattern of depth charges, bringing the enemy submarine to the surface. The HAGGARD rammed her at once, causing her to explode and sink, but leaving herself dead in the water. Her bow was pushed back two feet and three feet to starboard, both her shafts were out of alignment, and she was taking water through her sounding tubes. Presently, however, she reported that she was able to make 15 k, and at 0205 she was ordered to proceed to Ulithi with the UHLMANN, the latter to rejoin the formation on L-minus-7, if the HAGGARD was in shape to continue unescorted. COMDESDIV 94 received congratulations from COMFIFTHFLT.

"At 0340, another surface contact was made, and the COLOHAN was ordered to investigate. There was still another contact at 0413, and several more in the following hour, until at 0522, an enemy submarine surfaced 800 yards on the GUAM's port quarter. An emergency turn was ordered immediately, and the REMEY and TRATHEN were sent to the spot. A pattern of depth charges had no results."

So now we got subs chasing us.

Proff stopped by on his way up to the pilothouse, and we fell into a discussion of the difference between battleship duty and carrier duty. It came down to this, we agreed:

When you're in a battleship, you're in the Annapolis Navy. You feel that John Paul Jones and Admiral Dewey and Preble and Mahan and Farragut and all the rest of them are glaring at you, waiting to put you under hack because your shoelaces aren't tied with a false turk's-head knot, or some such nonsense.

But when you're in a carrier, you're in the fighting Navy. Your ship is being run by and for a bunch of barn-storming youngsters who don't tie their shoes at all, if they don't feel like it, and who would just as soon address Admiral King as "Ernie," unless it meant he'd ground them and keep them out of the next scrap.

Proff and I, we'll take carrier duty.

1245. The radars picked up a low, close bogey, so we were called to GQ. It had begun to rain, the ceiling was only 500 feet or so, and quite a sea had made up since morning. The *McCord* was goring the waves and tossing them over her shoulders as if they were red instead of pewter-colored. All around the horizon, ships were firing, but our personal bogey turned into a TBM carelessly approaching from the wrong sector.

Everybody seemed a little scatterbrained this afternoon. Jim Smith told me he'd heard an excited voice on TBS: "Hello, Russia! This is—— Out!" And a while later, an anxious young communications watch officer polled flag plot on whether we knew anything about "a dispatch to which the *Wisconsin* would have answered 'Negative.' "

There was more firing at 1630, when a destroyer reported sighting another low bogey, and still more when a couple of mines drifted through the formation, but except for the subs this morning, we were never really threatened all day.

For that matter, we didn't do much threatening on our own part. The target assigned us was Naha Airfield, on southwest Okinawa. TF 58 had planned to throw the high, hard one at it, but the weather became so foul, all strikes after the first were canceled. Our task group flew only 173 sorties, about half the usual number. Even so, we lost two F6s and their pilots to Naha's AA, and three TBMs, one F6, and one SC operationally, including the pilot and crew of one of the TBMs.

An operational loss can be caused by a mid-air collision, a landing crack-up, engine failure, or 50 other things. For instance, the SC (the Curtiss Seahawk, a seaplane) was lost when a wave capsized it as the pilot was trying to hook on to the *Missouri's* crane. I watched the whole thing. He barely had time to wipe the water out of his eyes before the *Colohan* was alongside, scooping him up.

Some of us will remember this ship as the "Fighting Lady," others as the "Lucky Y." But I sometimes think I'll remember her chiefly as the ship where the galley considered cold chopped spaghetti as a standard ingredient in a salad.

Two more boils tonight. Doc Lenhardt says my theory of their origin is ridiculous. He blames them on the wrong diet—too many carbohydrates. Maybe. . . .

After he had dressed them for me, he took me by to see the Jap prisoners who had been put aboard a few days ago. All three were wounded (one had lost a foot), all three were young, and all three had the same expression; i.e., none at all. They lay in their beds, staring at the overhead. They did not even glance at us when we came in or when we left. The Marine sentry said that none of the three ever looked anywhere near his direction.

Doc opened another door. "Here's an interesting case," he said. "This is Davis. How you coming, son?"

The boy said, "OK, thanks, Doc."

There was a cast on his left arm from the wrist to the shoulder, and bandages covered his whole chest and belly.

Doc asked, "Where's that little souvenir of yours?"

Davis reached under the bedclothes and pulled out a thick strip of metal about four inches wide and 18 inches long, heavy and curved and flanged.

"When they brought Davis in here," Doc told me, "two-thirds of this thing—whatever it is—was buried in his belly. He's a gunner's mate—third class, son?—third class, on that quad that took such a pasting from the bomb. This chunk here caught him across the arm, compound fracture, and then penetrated his belly. There wasn't more than six, seven inches of it sticking out. I don't know why he's alive today, unless it's that gunner's mates are naturally rugged. Reckon that's it, Davis?"

Davis tried to make his pleasant young face look tough. "That's it Doc!"

We went into the ward. "And here's Carveth," Doc said.

He had already told me about Carveth, the boy who had leaned out of a port just as the bomb exploded, and had taken the blast full in his face. One of his eyes had been removed, but there was a chance of saving some of the sight in the other; if a flashlight was pressed against it, he could tell whether it was lit. Two rubber tubes led from the bandages over the upper half of his face. The lower half was raw, red flesh, pitted black where the fragments had struck.

Doc straightened his pillow. "How you coming, Danny?"

Carveth's smile pulled your heart to pieces. "Coming fine, Doc! Just fine!"

As we walked back to Doc's office, he said, "Guts."

March 24th. At sea

This morning's air plan called for sixteen fighters to be launched at 0555. When the word was passed to man planes, the flight deck was still black, so Pappy Harshman told the plane captains to shout out their numbers, to help the pilots find them. Their voices floated up to the bridge, some deep, some shrill: "Nine! . . . Forty-six! . . . Thirty-four! . . . Seventeen! . . . Forty-one! . . ."

Buck yelled, "Bingo!"

"Sold American!" Red yelled.

Pilots have a proverb. "There are old pilots and bold pilots, but there are no old, bold pilots." Pappy Harshman is too old to fly combat now; he's 45, which is the same as having one foot in the grave, as far as combat flying is concerned. But from what other veterans tell me, he was white-hot stuff in his prime. One of them told me, "Pappy? Give him a shingle and an outboard motor, and he'd do slow rolls for you." One look betrays him to you: his whole face is tanned to the color of a saddle, except the areas around his eyes and the points of his jaws, which the sun couldn't reach through his goggles and chin strap. He got a lot of that burn drifting in a rubber raft off Panama.

Department of Utter Confusion on TBS this morning: "Hello, Quebec. Erase, erase, erase!"

Sometimes these call signs take you into a surrealist world. Here is a line from flag plot's log: "Dipsy Doodle reports many skunks bearing 209, 25 k." ("Skunk" is code for a surface contact, a companion term to "bogey" in the air.)

There are two reasons why everybody sprints for his battle station the instant General Quarters sounds. The sooner you get there, obviously, the sooner you can take up your duties. The second reason is, if you don't get there fast, you won't get there at all, because two minutes after the bugle has blown, every hatch and scuttle is bolted down, and every door is dogged tight, in order to confine fire, flooding, or other damage to the smallest possible area. This is called "Material Condition Afirm," but it might as well be "Still pond, no more moving!" Once Condition Afirm has been set, you're stuck. You can't go from one deck to another, or even to the next compartment. No one would dare violate the regulation, so I don't know what the penalty is, but I imagine it's something lingering, with boiling oil.

When attacks are possible but not imminent, Condition Afirm is relaxed to Condition Modified Afirm. The scuttles and doors are still bolted, but you're allowed to go through if you close them behind you promptly. If I want to get from my room to flag bridge during Modified Afirm, I have to wrench open seven heavy doors and one scuttle before I can get above the hangar deck. In addition, I have to pick my way through the damage-control parties that man the different compartments. They are posted to handle the fire hoses, shut off the valves, plug the ruptured pipes, and so on, if an emergency arises, but until then they have nothing to do but kill time.

Most of them sleep, curled up on the naked deck. Some play gin rummy, acey-deucey, or cribbage. Others sharpen their knives, write letters, or read (one of our mess attendants has been absorbed in *Strange Fruit*). Still others devote themselves to various kinds of scrim-shaw work—carving, engraving, weaving. There is a man in the compartment at the foot of the Exec's ladder who is as expert and delicate an embroiderer as I've ever seen.

The AA at Naha knocked down another of our planes today: an SB2C.

March 25th (Sunday). At sea

Chaplains do their best business on the Sundays before and after battles. There was no chance to hold services last Sunday; the ship was at General Quarters or Air Defense almost all day long. But today was a fueling day, and George Wright and Joe Moody had their biggest congregations since they've been aboard. George began his sermon, "Today is Palm Sunday. Last Sunday was Bomb Sunday."

Before Coop Bright sat down to lunch, he went up to Pat Patterson and said, "Good morning, Mr. Patterson, sir. I trust you're well today, sir. If there is anything I can do for you, sir, I hope you will let me know, sir. Thank you, sir!" And all through the meal he kept inviting Pat to "Try some of this jam, sir. . . . How about some fresh coffee, sir? . . . Sir, may I offer you a cigarette, sir?"

Such respectful solicitude was so unlike Coop, I asked him about it later. He said, "Didn't you hear what Pat did the other day? A low bogey was coming in, and just before he opened fire, he pulled air plot's key on the squawk-box and yelled, 'Southerners on yo' feet an' Yankees under the table! The battle's about to begin!' He held the key down all during the firing, and I want to tell you, you never heard such a goddam racket in your life! It sounded like every gun on the ship had moved into air plot. The Exec came out of his chair like he'd sat on a tack. Telephones jumped out of their cradles. Pencils rolled off the desk. You couldn't hear yourself think, and my ears rang for ten minutes after they'd knocked off firing. That big Texas bastard's got the sign on all of us, and he knows it! But I'm just treating him polite till I can dream up a way to get back at him."

It looks as if more men were lost on the *Franklin* than on any other single ship in all naval history. Every day, as they drain another compartment that had been flooded, they find another dozen or so bodies, and another dozen names are transferred from the "Missing in Action" roll to the roll of "Killed in Action." The present total is 772. The only warships I can think of that may have had worse casualties are the *Hood,* the *Repulse,* and the *Prince of Wales.*

It never occurs to you to ask a friend of yours in the Navy what he did in civilian life, and when he happens to tell you, you are almost always astonished: you could picture him in any job but the one he'd had. I'd known that Bill Ogdon wrote editorials for *The New York Times,* but tonight it transpired that he was a Bachelor of Divinity and had been a "traipsin' man" in the Kentucky hills. Not only that, but his mother was Ina Duley Ogdon, who wrote "Brighten the Corner Where You Are," "Carry Your Cross With a Smile," and several hundred other gospel songs. Well, Stew Lindsay breeds champion Dobermans. "Pop" Farr, an aviation machinist's mate in VB-9, was a Pennsylvania state trooper, and Val Valiquet, a pilot in VBF-9, was an adagio dancer. One of our enlisted photographers is Judge Landis's grandson. Another played in Leslie Howard's *Hamlet.* And I know a night-fighter pilot—a damn good one, too—who had been a welldigger; he'd quit because it was too dangerous.

Scraps: Four boils opened today. Wow! But think of Danny Carveth. . . .

Coop calls Wellington Henderson "the Man with the Million-Dollar Name." He says, "Get a name like that on your board of directors, and the suckers will break your door down!"

Wardroom definition of Annapolis: "A place where an innocent boy serves a four-year term, then spends the rest of his life committing crimes."

March 26th. At sea

I had to go to sick bay again this morning to get my dressings changed. On the way back, coming along the third deck, I smelled fresh bread and followed my nose into the bakeshop, remembering that I had overslept breakfast. The bakers seemed to welcome drop-in trade, because I had hardly taken a hungry, beseeching sniff before they produced two thick slices, buttered, a cup of smoking coffee, and a wedge of cake. It wasn't angel food cake, but an angel would have blasphemed to get the recipe, I told them so.

One of them said, "You just hit us on a good day." His name was Drum, a skinny youngster with flamboyant tattoos. "Most days, all we need to start the guns firing is to put a cake in the oven. The dough's made right, the cake begins to puff up pretty, and wham!, the 5-inchers begin walking the dog, and the cake falls flat on its face. It goes in sponge cake and it comes out pancake."

Another baker, Volk, said, "It's either the guns or a sea. Honest to God, I'm beginning to think we must of done something wrong somewheres, something we don't know nothing about, because we sure got somebody mad at us! You know how your batter is soft and runny one minute, and a minute later it's set firm? Well, say it's a dead calm when we put it in the oven. Before it can set, up comes a wind out of nowheres—*nowheres*—and what happens? The ship rolls, the batter runs to one end of the pans, and there it sets. The kind of cake you get, I wouldn't feed to a dogface—all soggy on the thick end and burnt black on the thin end. Whoever called this ocean 'Pacific'? It's about as pacific as a goddam roller coaster!"

Drum said, "We been lucky today, though. It's a good thing, because the air department notified us we got a landing coming up, so we have to give 'em a real Technicolor production. Want to see it?"

He displayed a cake so magnificent that you could have done Christies in its white expanse of icing. Lettered on it in pink was

USS YORKTOWN
21,000th LANDING
26 MARCH 1945

"Now *that*," Drum said proudly, "*that's* what *I* call a *cake*."

When a battleship or a cruiser or another carrier wants to deliver some papers or films to your ship, it stuffs them into a small bag of red and yellow bunting and assigns a pilot to skim over you and drop it on your deck—a trick that takes nice judgment in any sort of wind. Soon after lunch, Proff called flag plot on the squawk-box: "We've just landed an *Essex* TBM. Don't know what he wants." The Chief of Staff suggested, "Maybe he was trying to make a message-drop and flew too low."

Even Commander Jackson gave us a laugh. He posted a new and impenetrably complicated watch bill for the flag duty officers, with a note at the bottom: "Anyone who understands the system I use in this, please see me and explain it."

From the Plan of the Day: "We strike again today— We must remain alert at all times— Remember, it's team work with brain work." The strike cost our air group four planes. An F6 and a TBM collided over Okinawa; the pilot of the F6 got it down on the ground, so he may have survived, but the TBM crashed with its whole crew. Another F6 was knocked down by flak, and the third simply disappeared during a strafing run.

A couple of the TBS talkers on other ships are beginning to match their voices to their call signs. "Frankenstein" has adopted a bloodcurdling drawl, and "French Girl" speaks with a giggly twitter.

March 27th. At sea

If there is one poem I never want to read or hear again, it's the one that begins, "I stood on the bridge at midnight." We had about an hour's sleep between last night's Air Defense and GQ at 0245 this morning.

By now I'm pretty sharp at this quick-change routine. The secret is, leave your drawers in your trousers when you undress, and when you step into them, step into your shoes at the same time. Similarly, leave your shirt in your windbreaker. Keep your socks in one pocket and your muffler in another. You can zip and button yourself on the run, and knot your muffler and pull on your socks when you've reached the bridge.

No bogeys came close enough to make us open fire, and we secured at 0340. Paul Brogan, the Synthetic Gunnery Training officer, and Pat Garvan think the Japs are sending down these snoopers to keep us awake and soften us up for a hundred-plane raid later today.

Overheard on the hangar deck this afternoon: "He's a chief metalsmith—one of those old bastards with silver in his hair, gold in his teeth, and lead in his pants."

I'm getting back in the swing of reading dispatches, but every now and then I still come across a bit of Navy jargon that stumps me. The elementary stuff I can take in my stride: URDIS 241455 SEE MYDIS 220346 X (I'm making this one up, and any good communicator can probably pick holes in it) LT MICHAEL MIKE JONES USNR HEREDET CHARLIE ABLE 38 PROPEP ICOM MAKIN FURAS DUFLY— "In reply to your dispatch dated 2:55 pm on the 24th, I refer you to my dispatch dated 3:46 am on the 22nd. Lt. Michael M. Jones USNR is hereby detached from the USS *San Francisco* [CA 38] and will proceed and report to the Commander of Makin Island for further assignment to duty involving flying."

Anybody can read a message like that, given a little experience with the Navy's alphabet—Able, Baker, Charlie, Dog, and so on—and its system of taking the first syllables of the key words in a phrase and running them together to form an over-all word. Thus, for dispatch purposes, "Commander of Carrier Division 6" becomes COMCARDIV 6; "Commander of Naval Aircraft in the South Pacific" becomes COMAIRSOPAC; and Commander of Service Forces in the Atlantic" becomes COMSERFORLANT. These are simple agglutinations, easy to break apart and restore to full pomp. Moreover, they are pronounceable. But how about CNAOPTRA? You may know that he's the Chief of Naval Operational Training, but what are you going to call him?—Frankie? Philip Guedalla once complained of "the anfractuosities of Basque nomenclature." I bet he'd have broken his teeth on "CNAOPTRA."

Say that by now you're fairly fluent in reading dispatches. You know the difference between CAP and SAP (a combat air patrol and a semi-armor-piercing bomb); between CMM and CMA (a chief machinist's mate and a comma); between CAVU and ATTU (ceiling and visibility unlimited and Escort Carrier Number 102); and between AO and AOL (a fleet tanker and absent over leave). Well, you're still no more than halfway toward complete comprehension. You still have to familiarize yourself with local geography. You don't want to get SADO confused with JATO, do you? Sado is an island on the west coast of Honshu; Jato is jet-assisted take-off. Or BUNGO with MINGO? Bungo Strait separates Shikoku and Kyushu; the *Mingo* is a submarine. And when you happen across KIA, you should be aware that there's a town by that name in China, before you assume that the sender meant "killed in action."

In the early part of the War, an officer told me, "I've fought at Buna, Buin, Buka, and Bupers, and the Bupers fight was the worst of the four." Buna is in New Guinea; Buin and Buka, in Bougainville; Bupers is the Navy's Bureau of Personnel.

The *New Jersey* has just joined our task group. She seems delighted with her call sign, "Werewolf," because she's been keeping the TBS busy with messages uttered in a throaty howl. "Frankenstein" still has the grisliest voice, though, with "Sharkfin" a snappy second.

March 28th. At sea

This morning we took aboard fuel, mail, and ammunition. It was the first time we had rearmed at sea, and some of the men were rather apprehensive. We'd send a heavy wire net across to our AE, the *Wrangell,* her working party would tumble a dozen big bombs into it, and we'd haul it back, swaying and grinding. If our crane operator misjudged the roll of the ship, the whole netload of TNT would slam into our side or onto the deck. I knew the bombs weren't fused, but they gave me the clatters all the same.

Right in the middle of the fueling, one of our destroyers got a sound contact with a submarine, 2000 yards dead ahead. The weasel in the hen house! But the contact didn't develop.

Scraps: An ironic sentence from the dispatch board: TWO PERFECT NAPALM HITS WERE MADE ON A CHURCH.
Today's scuttlebutt: The Jap fleet is on its way to meet us.

From the Plan of the Day: "You were informed before leaving Ulithi that our estimate of what we might expect from the Jap was an unknown quantity. Since then four carriers have been hit. Our days will be long—they will be tiring —they will be tough. While we all may be 'Dead Tired' let's not get *dead* from being *tired.* WE MUST BE ALERT—WE MUST THINK AND WORK TOGETHER."

March 29th. At sea

1415. Sneak attack! I was on flag bridge, waiting for the

bugle to blow "secure," when the guns began to hammer, and a thick column of mottled water spouted high in the air, 50 feet off our port quarter. The navigating bridge blotted most of my overhead view, but I caught a flash of the plane that had dropped the bomb, as it fled away—a low-mid-wing, single-engine monoplane, with a tail assembly like an F6's. This is all I saw, and all I could report to flag plot, before I had to duck; the muzzles of Number 2 turret were staring me full in the face.

(Later: This plane *was* an F6. The column of water had been thrown up not only by a bomb, but also by the bogey, which had plunged in with its bomb still attached. In fact, the blast had hurled pieces of the shattered plane up on our deck—that's why the column had looked mottled. One of the cylinders lit in Dick Tripp's safey net, and other fragments riddled two SB2Cs near by.)

In all the lather, I forgot that we had been steaming through an archipelago of floating mines, until I saw a destroyer stop dead in the water and fire at one for what seemed ten minutes. No explosion. Hendy, whom a mere *kamikaze* doesn't disturb in the least, watched the destroyer back down, then creep up on the mine again. "Maybe he's desperate and is going to ram it," Hendy said.

Scraps: In any crowd of sailors, you'll always find a few "hard rocks" who cock their caps over their left eyebrows. Occasionally you'll find one who wears his helmet the same way. I saw such a one swaggering down the flight deck this afternoon, just before the attack. When he got back to his unsteady feet, all his strut was gone; he put his helmet on straight.

I don't understand the atmospheric condition that causes it, but when our planes were taking off today, double spirals of vapor curled from the tips of their props.

Good Friday services tonight. George Wright had on the first necktie I've seen since I came aboard, and I noticed for the first time that what I'd thought was a haloed cross on the lectern cloth is actually a compass rose.

The word is that a typhoon is due to pass close to Okinawa four days from now. I hope the *Loy** misses it. I hate to think of a little APD in one of those blows. . . .

---

*My brother was her exec at the time. An APD is an escort destroyer converted to a fast transport.

From the Plan of the Day: "For us it's back deep into 'Indian Country'—the prize, the Jap Fleet and shipping—a choice target— Heads up!"

March 30th. At sea

GQ this morning caught me with pants down, literally. I was in sick bay, having my boils dressed again—five of them, now. The talker reported "One to three bogeys, 8 miles, closing." I didn't think I could make it up those seven ladders before they reached us, but I lit a shuck anyhow. Puffing, I flung myself against the tape only to see Joe Hurley, the new Flag Lieutenant, taking off his helmet.

"Bogey was a friendly," he said.

Bob Doyle, the flag ACIO, showed me some new stereo photographs of Izumi Airfield. It gives you a godlike feeling to peer down on a three-dimensional landscape that you could hold in your hand. Automobiles, planes, houses, trees, all were so brilliantly clear in even their smallest details, you itched to touch them. A factory chimney was no larger than the stem of a clay pipe. Those zigzag trenches—a child had squiggled a sharp stick through the dust. Bomb craters were the tiny lairs where sand crabs hide. The skeleton of a burnt-out hangar was as delicate as a spider web. Another building might have been made of thin pastry; a mouse might have gnawed the bomb hole in its roof. One wipe of your finger, and the whole fragile miniature would be demolished.

Bob said, "Hey! you'll smudge 'em!"

Halfway through the afternoon watch, TBS suddenly shouted, "Hello, Russia! This is Comanche! I have a contact bearing 065, 700 yards!" The Admiral ordered "Emergency Turn 9!", and the whole huge task group spun on its heel. We waited tensely for another report, wondering if it would be a torpedo's, but Comanche kept silent; her contact must have been false. (For some reason, she pronounces her call sign "Com-manch," just as Tortoise calls herself "Tortoys.")

March 31st. At sea

GQ at dawn. I was ashamed to be so stale and musty on so beautiful a morning. The sky was fresh-scrubbed, fresh-painted. The only clouds were small ones, low and far away, shaped like a French loaf. The rising sun sparkled from the super-structures of the battleships, as if they were steaming in a poster by Anton Otto Fischer. An *Essex*-class carrier on the horizon southwest of us began to blink with a searchlight of a diamond brilliance that drilled into my still-drowsy eyes, I closed them and turned away, but I popped them wide open when I heard Pappy Harshman on the bull horn: "Keep the area of the 5-inch mounts clear! They may have to fire across the deck!"

Flag plot had given us no warning, so I called them on the tube. As usual, they had forgotten to unlatch their end. Wolfe went in to tell them and came back with the word: "Seven bogeys, 40 miles on our starboard quarter."

Forty miles at 250 knots—call it ten minutes. Five minutes passed. . . . The tube murmured, "Bogeys closing!" Another five minutes. . . . "Bogey has been identified as an Oscar, 9 miles dead astern!" But almost at once the bugle rang out, the whistle blew, and Babe Herman announced, "Set Condition 1 Easy in all AA batteries! Materiel Condition Moddafied Afoim!" I guess our CAP caught the Oscar and splashed him, but I never found out.

There was another GQ around 1045, as we were landing a patrol, but again we secured without having to fire. Coop put the explanation on the tape:

LAST., G., 1., Q, XXXX G.Q. WAS DUE TO COZY PLANES RETURNING., ON THE WRONG APPROACH PRODE, CEDURE. CAP THAT JUST LANDED HAD NO WAVEOFFS ., ADVERAGE INTERVIL, 24 SECONDS. LANDING SIGNALS OFFICER SAYS "VERY GODDL," . . . SNACK SHOP ONE UNDER NEW MANAGEMENT-TRY ONE., OF MILLERS HAM SNAWHICH WITH MAN, YOMAISE.,..,.

Jim Smith is being recommended for a Bronze Star, and the Admiral has detailed Hendy and me to compose the citation. It struck us both that here might be a very pretty little racket. Why not let Jim compose it himself?—at a price? For a mere $2, we would let him pick an adjective out of stock— "resourceful," "indefatigable," "painstaking," "indispensable" —or give him his choice of three for $5. Of course, this rate would apply only to the hackneyed old stuff that appears in every citation, even the hush-dears that incompetent admirals get when they're plucked out of the wreckage of their commands. For a really distinguished tribute, we figured Jim would be willing to dig a little deeper. We worked out a tentative scale—$3 for "suave," $4.25 for "witty," $25 for "handsome"—and offered him our proposition. The high-minded swine wouldn't touch it!

The boys at Radiotokyo are hitting the hop again. Their fantasia this afternoon takes the rag off'n the bush:

"The enemy task force is still roving the waters around Okinawa Jima, but is being subjected to heavy losses by Japanese air units aided by units of the Imperial Navy. Since the task force entered these waters, it has lost thirty-odd warships. Confirmed results are as follows: one battleship sunk, nine battleships heavily damaged, six cruisers sunk, one minesweeper sunk, two transports sunk, and a number of unidentified ships left in flames. These devastating attacks are being carried [*sic*] by Japanese Special Attack Corps, who leave their bases on a one-way mission of death and destruction for the enemy.

"During the enemy's B-29 attack on the Japanese home islands on March 26th, Sub-Lieutenant Kay accounted for fourteen of the giant bombers. Said Sub-Lieutenant Kay, quote, I have found the weak spot of the enemy's Superfortress, and with one burst of my guns, the engines fly to pieces, unquote."

Sounds as if Kay had been there, too, when the hop was passed.

2400. March went out like a lamb. . . .

April 1st (Easter Sunday). At sea. L-Day at Okinawa

—But April came in like a lion: Air Defense sounded at 0130. On the way up the ladders, a sailor tore past me yelling, "I'm the only son of a bitch in the whole son-of-a-bitchin' fleet can put his socks on at a full gallop! And that ain't all, either! I——" he popped down a passageway like the White Rabbit, and I lost the rest of it.

For once, flag plot was almost deserted. Only three officers were there: the Chief of Staff, as always (he must sleep there, standing up), and Stew Lindsay, and Jim Smith, who had the duty. The Admiral stumbled in, yawning and rubbing his eyes. Jim told him, "One bogey, sir—180, 40 miles," and Stew brought him a summary of the TBS reports, crossing the

99

compartment with the apprehensive stoop of a tall man under a low overhead.

We were waiting for further news from CIC when I suddenly realized that this was Easter; Lent had ended, I could smoke again! I bummed a cigarette from Stew. In the middle of my coughing fit, someone shouted, "Splash one Betty, 290, 20!" and we all stampeded for the bridge. An orange flame wavered down slowly, touched the sea, and faded to a glow.

The Admiral said, "That'll teach him!"

Back to the sack at 0150, thinking what a slave's life this is. Twenty-four hours a day, we're on more peremptory call than a doctor. There's not a single future minute to which I can point and promise myself, "When such-and-such a time arrives. I'll do thus-and-so." I may put a spoonful of sugar in my coffee, and stir it, but I have no assurance that I'll ever drink it. Even as I lift the cup (or take a pencil from my pocket, or unbutton my trousers), a radar monitor in CIC may spot a sudden flicker in the green ribbons that flow across his screen. "Forty miles," he'll say. "Closing. Better turn 'em out!" and the bugler will spit the four C's—"dit, *dah!* dit, *dah!*" that open air defense, or the F,F,F,C of general quarters.

Coop and I were taking a breather on the flight deck after dinner, and Pat Patterson bellowed down to him, "Hey, Bright, put on your cap! You're two-thirds naked!"

Hendy and I had the afternoon watch. The task group was quiet, and the Admiral was in his sea cabin, so we passed the time playing April Fool. Bob Doyle bit on a fake phone message, Jones on an imaginary rip in his pants, a Marine orderly on an untied shoelace. We fixed up one for the Chief of Staff, though, that we thought was really funny. While he was out on the bridge, we borrowed a red crayon and colored the tips of four or five butts in his ash tray. Luck was with us. He came back with a cigarette, walked straight to the ash tray, and looked at the red butts. The moment he spoke, we were ready to bombard him with accusations. But he didn't speak. He didn't smile. He didn't show any expression whatsoever. He just looked. After a long minute he said gravely, "Not mine," and picked up the dispatch board. Curtain.

From the Plan of the Day: "This is Easter Day. Followers of Christ everywhere are thinking of the events of Passion

Week which culminate in His glorious Resurrection. We find ourselves engaging a bitter, relentless enemy, even on this Day dedicated to the Prince of Peace. Two thousand years ago, as today, force was on the throne, having crucified the Son of God. But the Resurrection was God's answer to force! This was the victory of faith which overcame the world.

"Donald Hankey, of World War I fame, said that religion was betting your life there was a God. Well, he did and won. We need that kind of faith this Easter Day.
                                            "The Chaplains."

In my room I found a beautiful cake on my desk. Bob Lawrence said, "Your friends from the bake shop left it here." I guess it represents the thousandth time that Commander Jackson has landed on me.

April 2nd. At sea

I wish I'd kept track of how much shut-eye I've averaged in the past several nights. I bet it wouldn't top five hours. Take last night: asleep at 0100; awake at 0330, when the telephone called Bob for the morning watch; back to sleep a few minutes later; and awake for good when Air Defense blew at 0415, with GQ immediately afterwards.

CIC had been a little slow in turning us out. The task group to starboard was firing already, and I had hardly buckled my helmet when there was a flash of sulphurous light and a peal of thunder from a battleship in our own task group. I reported it to flag plot: "A battleship dead ahead of us has opened fire."

Flag plot asked, "A battleship in this formation?"

Short sleep makes short tempers. I was on the point of yelling into the tube, "If she wasn't in this formation, how the hell could I see she was a battleship?" I choked it back, though, and answered, "Affirmative."

The firing slackened and died, and, still we stayed at our stations. I ached for sleep, but the east was paling when we secured.

From the Plan of the Day: "The troops that landed at Okinawa yesterday depend upon us to maintain control of the air. It will be done!"

There's not much doubt about who has controlled it so far. The joint B-29-carrier strikes against the Honshu airbases in the last couple of weeks must have cost the Japs

101

close to a thousand planes, either shot down or destroyed on the ground. In fact, the conviction that Jap air power is crippled, at least temporarily, is so general that Torpedo 9 has finally agreed to let me fly a few of their missions—something their skipper, Tom Stetson, would hesitate to allow if heavy interception were probable.

Their ACIO, Dick Montgomery, told me to be in Ready 4 at 1000, to fill out the gaps in my gear. All I owned was a flying suit—the one Joe Mayer had given me—and a knife, a flashlight, and a pair of gloves, so I had to borrow a helmet, a life jacket, and a parachute. The pilots and most of the crewmen carried pistols, but a pistol is too personal to be borrowed; I didn't ask for one.

Bob Fulton, who was flying me, put a recording of "Duffy's Tavern" on the Victrola and stretched out in his chair. He said, "I must have heard that damn thing a hundred times, but it still gives me a laugh."

"Laugh?" another pilot said. *"Laugh?* Me, I'm as nervous as an ignorant bridegroom."

Around 1100 the ticker started to rattle and jerk: PILOTS MAN YOUR——

"Hubba-hubba!" they shouted. "Hubba-hubba, gang!" We crowded out to the catwalk, climbed to the flight deck, and ran to our TBM's for all the world like a football team taking the field.

"This is Gardner, my radioman," Bob said. "He'll square you away. Call me if you need anything." He jumped up on the starboard wing and climbed into his cockpit.

Gardner opened the door to the tunnel. I said, "You're the radioman? That means I've got to ride the turret?"

"Yes, sir."

The turret of a TBM is about the size of a kettledrum, and although I've never curled up in a kettledrum, it couldn't help being the more comfortable choice. The ideal turret-gunner is built like a jockey; I'm a shade over 6 feet 2. . . . I squirmed into the seat and doubled my knees under my chin, trying to work my feet against the rests. No dice; my legs had to hang. Then I tried to settle myself. Still no dice; the breech of the .50 gun left me no more room than the Hindu boy in the sword-basket trick, and every time I wriggled, I snagged some part of my gear on a protruding bolt or lug. I have never worried about getting wounded on a mission, or having to jump; but I have always been terrified of being trapped, pinned, in the plane. And there I was. . . .

"Start engines!" I couldn't tell when ours started. Its in-

102

dividual roar was lost in the mass roar. I could feel the plane quiver, but that might have been caused by the slipstream of the one in front of us. Behind us was TBM Number 134, so close that its propeller was almost chopping our flipper. A crewman caught the pilot's eye and made the gesture that ordinarily accompanies a description of a voluptuous figure, but here it was the signal for him to shut his bomb-bay doors. An ordnanceman fixed four rockets under our wings. The *Yorktown* began turning left into the wind, and the *Wisconsin* appeared on our port quarter. (I had never noticed before that, from this target angle, an *Iowa*-class battleship looks exactly like a monstrous crab.) Our plane began to move, taxi-ing into take-off position. The wings spread out and snapped into place. I heard Fulton's voice: "Check IFF." Then Gardner's: "IFF is on, sir." Then Fulton's again: "We're down, goddam it! No VHF. *Je*-sus!" (IFF is a radar device— "Identification of Friend or Foe"; VHF is the Very High Frequency radiophone.)

A handling crew folded our wings and shoved us to Number 3 elevator, which sank into the gloom of the hangar deck, where we were wheeled off and chocked. When I tried to slip down from the turret, I couldn't. My flying suit and chute straps were caught. Gardner had to help me unsnag them. I was trembling when I crawled out on the deck.

"Sorry this happened," Bob said, "but don't worry; we'll get it fixed in time for the sweep this afternoon. I guess we've missed lunch. How about some soup and a sandwich in the ready room?"

We ate and smoked and waited, watching Coop scatter his nonsense through the air department's bulletins on the ticker: FRIENDLY PLANES IN THE AREA INCLUDE PBM,,. PB4Y2, OS2U, SC AND CARRIER TYPES .,.TIME 1308 ,..,. MY DARLING WEASEL:, THE OBJECT IS TO EXECUTE THE INSTRUCTIONS., AS ORDERED OR THE FLAT OF MY FOOT ACROSS YOUR HAIRY PUSS,. SIGNED ONE WHO HATES YOU. Neither Bob nor I knew who Weasel was. Eventually our flight was called: SWE,EP 2 PILOTS HUBBA HUBBA. TIEM 1458.,., VT & VB PILOTS MAN YOUR PLANES.

Gardner had been relieved by a turret-gunner, Fries, so I was to ride in the bilges. Fries made sure I knew how to load the little .30 stinger gun. When he was satisfied, he told me, "Hold tight and brace yourself when you're changing position, or you're liable to get a bad bump if the plane jinks. One hand for the plane, and one for yourself." He scampered into the turret like a squirrel, tucked up his legs, and raised the armor plate. The side toward me was stenciled HARD HOMO. A free translation, I thought, might be "tough hombre."

I plugged in my earphones, latched my safety belt, and adjusted my shoulder straps. The plane jerked and waddled, slowly at first, then the flight deck began to slide under us, faster and faster. We shot off the bow, and suddenly I was looking up at the ramp. I braced myself for the shock of a crash into the sea: *He that flies so will ne'er return again!* But the ramp came level with us. The ship fell astern.

There was no compass in the bilges and no clock, nothing but radio instruments, a thermometer, and an altimeter. When we reached 500 feet, I threw off my belt and straps, and buckled my chute harness. TBM 124 crept up on our port wing, rocking gently, and 128 closed in to starboard. There weren't more than two or three feet, it seemed, between our wing tips. If we had worn a brass ring on ours, 128 could have hooked it with his Pitot tube. Three more TBMs were slightly astern and slightly below, and another three were ahead. Four F6Fs covered each flank of our formation, weaving mile-long garlands of vapor.

We kept climbing. The radio broke into hoarse cackles and squeals: "Hello, 390 Regent. This is Regent Base. What is your Easy Tare Able? Over."

"Hello, Regent Base. This is 390 Regent. My Easy Tare Able is shackle Mike George Prep Xray unshackle. Over."

"Roger, 390. Out."

The clouds thickened. They seemed to float past the side ports, but seen through the stinger port, they streaked past. When we reached 2200 feet, they were solid beneath us, and the glare was blinding. The shadows of our three-plane section, each "gloried" with a rainbow, were grouped like the three crowns on the Swedish royal standard.

A mumble on the radio became loud and clear: "I only carry certain packets of film, and—"

A hard voice broke in angrily, "Get off this channel with that talk!"

Another voice: "Hello, 308 Stratford. This is Banjo. Over. . . . Hello, 308 Stratford. This is Banjo. Over. . . ." The voice became anxious: "Hello, 308 Stratford! This is Banjo! Over! . . ." Then it said sadly, "Hello, Three-Zero-Eight Stratford or Three-Zero-*Nine* Stratford. This is Banjo. Over. . . ." No one answered.

Altitude, 3100 feet. Fulton waggled his wings in answer to a signal I had missed. I peered through the ports, expecting enemy planes, or a quick pushover, but there was nothing in sight except the clouds and our own planes. We roared on, still climbing.

The radio: "—Composition of my group is as follows: I have four chickens with 500-pound bombs, four chickens with 200-pound bombs, eight hawks with—" The voice faded away.

Something glittered through a slit in the clouds; we were still over the sea. But almost at once the clouds broke, and Okinawa was beneath us—a dainty island with crumpled hills, thickly wooded, sloping down to a neat crazy quilt of tan and green farmland. A village swept under our port wing. Half the houses had red tile roofs; the rest were thatched. I saw a yellow beach with a toothpick jetty, and then we were over the sea again. The chart showed that we had crossed the island at its narrow waist, where it is only two miles wide. The worst fighting was south of us, on our port hand. The formation headed there.

Now the landmarks became clear: Yontan Airfield, already ours; further south, Machinato Field; still further, the main field at Naha. The bay between Yontan and Machinato was not named on the chart, but "New San Francisco Bay" or "Little Hampton Roads" would have served: it was packed with hundreds of our ships—battleships, cruisers, transports, destroyers, cargo ships, LSTs—so many that they hardly had room to maneuver. The big warships were close inshore. One of their heavy guns would spurt flame, and seconds later, miles inland, a tower of smoke would rise. Offshore the destroyers idled around, like a touch alley-gang with their hands in their pockets, hoping for an excuse to pick a fight. I spotted an APD and wondered if she was the *Loy*. I couldn't read her number; the vibration of the plane jiggled my glasses too much.

The SB2Cs broke off and began to spiral upward. Fulton waggled his wings, and 124 crossed over from port and fell into line astern. The altimeter spun counterclockwise: 2700 feet, 2000, 1400, 900. . . . I knew that this was the usual preliminary to an attack, but I hadn't heard the air-ground coordinator assign us a target. I tapped my phones: the plugs had fallen out of the jack. I must have pulled them apart when I was twisting around, sight-seeing. I found it and shoved it home in time to hear Fulton say, "Stand by to strafe!"

I crawled over the seat, straddled the stinger gun, pinched its clip to free it, and loaded it. *They had tails like unto scor-*

pions, and there were stings in their tails. (Come to think of it, the verse also fits a TBM: *They had breastplates, it were breastplates of iron: and the sound of their wings was as the sound of chariots of many horses running to battle.*)

Fries broke into this scriptural orgy with, "I wouldn't sit like that, sir. Those shells come out pretty hot and they'll catch your ankle." The only alternative was to kneel, leaning over, as if I were going to be beheaded. I turned to glance at the altimeter: 700 feet, 600, 500. . . . As we shot across the beach, a flock of white birds scattered away from us. Columns of smoke from burning villages stood like stalagmites in the still air. F6s and F4Us were swarming, diving, strafing on every side. Under the wings of one plunging F6, two sparks flashed, and far in front of it two rockets smashed into a hillside with a twinkle and an explosion of gray dust. A napalm bomb hit squarely in the middle of a village; oily smoke boiled up from a dark red flame that ate outwards like a sore.

I crouched over the little .30, searching the terrain for something to strafe. Once I thought I saw a machine gun winking at us and some tracers streaking past, but I couldn't be sure. Otherwise, there was nothing—no troops, no trenches, no emplacements, no vehicles—nothing but deserted villages and empty roads.

Other planes were having the same trouble. A voice said, "Can't anybody give me a target? I've got to leave here in a few minutes."

"This is 201 Ruler. All I got all afternoon is one miserable sampan!"

"This is 99 Ripper. I saw a horse back there. Want his co-ordinates on the grid?"

A new voice: "There's a bridge to port. Guess we might as well dump on that."

"Hold it!" someone shouted. "Don't hit those bridges! They want to keep 'em intact."

Still another voice: "Where are all these caves we've been hearing about? We can lay our bombs in their mouths."

Bob called me: "You seen any caves?"

"Negative."

"Me either. I haven't seen a damn thing, on the ground or in the air. The Admiral's going to be plenty browned off when we get back. We supposed to land aboard at 1730, and it's 1655 now. Well, I'm going to let ding on the first thing I see."

Evidently the co-ordinator had not assigned targets today. The plane slowed suddenly as the bomb-bay doors opened. I peered through the bomb port, and saw two 500-pounders drop, and felt two bumps. Smoke and dust spread over a village behind us. I pressed the button of the mike: "Brother, you sure bull's-eyed that one!"

Bob said, "Yeah. . . . Whoa! There's a little bridge down here. I don't think I can get enough dive in, but I'm going to try to hit the son of a bitch anyhow. Nobody would use this one but a Jap."

We climbed steeply to 1300 feet. The doors opened again, and again I felt two bumps. Two huge columns of smoke and mud jumped high above the bridge, completely screening it. Neither Fries nor I could tell whether they were hits or near misses. We reported it to Bob. "The hell with it," he said. "Let's go home."

We dropped to 700 feet and headed for the eastern coast. Just before we came to it, Fries asked, "Any chance for any strafing, Mr. Fulton?"

"Negative. We're late now."

"I've got one round still in my gun. OK to fire it now before the join-up?"

"Affirmative."

There was a *pop,* and the smell of powder drifted down into the bilges.

Bob said sourly, "We might as well not have come over here, for all the good we did. . . . Well, secure all guns. Light up a cigarette, if you want to."

I took the belt out of the .30, emptied the chamber, and clipped the breech back to the tripod. "I'm going to take off my helmet," I told Bob. "Rock the wings if you want to call me, and I'll put it back on."

"Roger."

The cigarettes were in my knee pocket—I'd mashed them, huddled over the gun; and the matches sputtered—I'd sweated onto the box. But I got one lit, and propped my feet on the forward bulkhead, and bit off a piece of hard chocolate. It was cool without the tight helmet and quiet without the snarling phones. The flight unrolled in recollection: take-off, bombs, return. I tried to find something unusual in it, something to parade in conversation and in letters, but I couldn't. We had demolished a village and maybe a bridge, but the utter lack of opposition made it savorless. One machine gun, and doubtful at that. . . .

The under sides of the clouds were turning red. It was getting late. I pulled my helmet on in time to hear Fries say, "Two destroyers out to port, sir."

Bob answered, "They're the picket cans."

Another destroyer appeared under our starboard wing, and to port I saw the task group turning into the wind. Our wheels jolted down. We began a long, gliding turn. I shucked off my chute harness and gathered my shoulder straps and safety belt. The plane slowed; Bob had opened his flaps. There was still no hurry: he'd have to make three or four circles before Dick Tripp waved him in. Suddenly Dick's fluorescent suit glowed through the port, and we hit and jerked to a violent stop—so violent that a chest-pack parachute broke its lashings on the overhead and scored a direct hit on my right knee. When our wheels had been chocked, I stepped out on deck, and the numb knee gave way, and I fell flat, and at last the mission had achieved distinction.

The ship was at General Quarters, but I hobbled down to Ready 4 with Bob for the interrogation. Dick Montgomery was asking the pilot who had landed in front of us, "See anything?"

"Not much. There was this little river—don't ask me where —anyhow, one part of its channel is now 40 feet deeper."

Another pilot announced proudly, "*I* saw a man!"

The others crowded around him. "The hell you did! Did you strafe him?"

"Naw. He was on crutches."

"Why, you goddam softy!" they shouted. "They're high-priority targets, cripples and pregnant women!"

At supper, everybody was as happy as a bee-martin with a fresh bug, as the Carolina boys say. The word had been passed that we were fueling tomorrow, so 24 hours of relaxation were on the cards. Coop felt chipper enough to renew his feud with Pat Patterson. He waited till Pat had a mouthful of dessert, then called down the table, "Say, Pat, my grampaw told me the easiest part of the whole war was the march from Atlanta to the sea!"

Before Pat had stopped choking, Coop had gone.

April 3rd. At sea

I didn't hear about it until this morning, but the task group had an ugly collision last night. According to our log, the first word came at 2114, when the *New Jersey* announced, with what strikes me as rather haughty unconcern, "Hello,

Russia. This is Werewolf. We have just hit a destroyer. Returning to base course."

The destroyer was the *Franks*. She was changing station, and in the darkness and foul weather, she smashed into the *New Jersey* port bow, almost head on. The *New Jersey* reported, ALL DAMAGE NEGLIGIBLE X MINOR PLATE CRACK NEAR MAIN DECK EDGE X SHIP'S FORCE WILL EFFECT REPAIRS X NO PERSONNEL INJURIES. But the little *Franks* took a terrific beating. The *Jersey's* tremendous bow anchor scraped along her side and demolished everything in its path—the wing of the bridge, Number 4 quad and its director, the motor whaleboat and its director, the motor whaleboat and its davits. The stacks were buckled, the port torpedo director and its firing system were knocked out, and a dozen plates along the waterline sprang leaks. Her exec's summary of the damage was, "The ship is in no condition to complete the operation." The Medical officer's report was still worse: the Captain had a fractured femur and several fractured ribs, and the Comm officer, who was O.O.D. at the time of the collision, had multiple head lacerations, probable skull fracture, a brain injury, and a fractured right shoulder.

The *Franks* is famous in our task group for the eagerness with which she acknowledges all orders on TBS: "This is Gimlet! *Wil*-co! Out!", but when we detached her this afternoon, her farewell "Wilco" was so doleful that the men in flag plot shook their heads and said sadly, "Poor old Gimlet! She's lost her spirit. . . ."

Admiral Mitscher warned us two days ago, "Look out for storms as well as Japs." The weather has been making up since last night, and this morning we caught the edge of a real typhoom. The seas were slap heaps, heaving and crumbling. A 45-knot wind drove the rain at us like a barrage of BB-shot. The *Yorktown* did snap-rolls, wingovers, and Immelmanns. A fine day for sack drill—for spending a few hours in what Paul Brogan calls his "Simmons trainer."

1410. More trouble! The TBS suddenly announced, "Hello, Russia! This is Armada! Man overboard!" ("Armada" is the *Missouri*.)

The Admiral ordered, "Mark him with a smoke float!", then asked, "Who's astern of Armada?"

Commander Jackson glanced at the chart of our cruising disposition and picked up the phone: "Hello, Mountain!

Hello, Fishwife! Hello, Curio! Watch for man overboard from Armada!"

Armada said, "Hello, Mountain. Man is on my port quarter, about a hundred yards from you." And a few minutes later she added, "In addition to smoke float, man was marked with green dyemarker. A yellow life jacket is believed to be within 170 yards of him."

Mountain told her cheerily, "Have man in sight."

I looked through the port. The wind and sea were so wild, I had small hope that Mountain could get a line to him, much less that he could cling to it. But presently we heard, "Hello, Russia. Hello, Armada. This is Mountain. Man recovered. Details by visual. Out." He had been in the water exactly 22 minutes.

We were scheduled to fuel this morning, but the weather forced us to put it off. Toward the middle of the afternoon, however, the Admiral decided to attempt it anyway, running downwind. Fueling means mail. To be sure, COMSERFOR Ulithi had notified us that heavy seas had prevented him from loading mail for delivery today, but scuttlebutt knew better, as usual, and hands lined our starboard side as we overhauled the tanker, looking for the big gray bags. A tarpaulin was stretched across a pile of something on her deck. . . .

(Later: It wasn't mail.)

After supper, I went down to sick bay to read to Danny Carveth, the boy who had been blinded by the bomb. In the next bed was Moore, a mess attendant with pneumonia; a saline and glucose solution was draining into his right arm. He said he wanted to listen too, so I pulled up a chair between them. I had combed the wardroom library for something light and gay, and Bob Hope's *I Never Left Home* seemed to be just the dish, but as I read along, I began to doubt my choice: there were too many references to such esoterica as "the 21 Club" and "playing split weeks." I worried until it occurred to me that, for all I knew, Carveth was the darling of 21's headwaiters, and Moore had starred at the Palace.

(Three hours later: The stench from Carveth's cast still lingers in my shirt.)

April 4th. At sea

The *Yorktown* bucked like a rogue stallion all night long.

110

When I shaved this morning, I had to hold on to the basin with one hand; and when I crossed the compartment, half the distance was a climb, the other half a charge. The skies were clear, except for a spatter of small clouds as black as 40mm bursts, but the wind still blew a gale, and the seas were heavier than ever. Every time I watched one of our destroyers corkscrew over a crest, I pitied the *Franks's* skipper and Comm officer, with their jagged bone-ends grinding. Our two CVLs rolled so severely, I expected the planes on their flight decks to break their lashings and topple onto their wing tips. The rudders of our own planes were chocked to keep them from slatting, and when we catapulted two fighters, they jumped into the roaring air as if from a springboard.

Proff told me at breakfast that he had been in the pilot-house around 0400 when we hit a wave that brought us up short. Everybody was knocked flat. Captain Combs bounced out of his sea cabin shouting, "Who had the PPI?"

"I did, sir," Proff said.

"Well, my God, are you sure that was a wave and not a *ship?*"

Weather and all, we had to complete our fueling and take on a supply of ammunition. It must have been rugged on the working parties. Every few minutes, someone would report that a hose or a line had carried away, and once a 500-pound bomb was jerked from its sling and lost. There was a bonus, though. Our AE, the *Lassen,* brought us a big batch of mail, including a note from my brother, now somewhere off Okinawa, rounding out his thirtieth month at sea: "I have no hope of getting home unless the ship is lost, but the chances of that are considerable. These *kamikazes*—"*

Coming back from mail call, I heard an empty-handed sailor grumble, "My girl writes me regularly. Yep, every six months."

A drab day like this reminds you once again of a carrier's meager palette. Gray, blue, white, khaki—these are its basic colors, and so rare is any other that when I find it, I'm tempted to stop and bask (always excepting the sulphur yellow of a 5-incher's muzzle flash). Dick Tripp's fluorescent "zoot suit" is orange and red. The battle lights are a brilliant vermilion. The SB2Cs have pea-green spinners. But when you've seen these three, you've about exhausted our resources. Next time

---

*On the night of 28 May 1945, his ship, the *Loy,* shot down six *kamikazes* in 12 hours. The sixth hit the water so close aboard that it ricocheted into her side, setting fires and killing 15 men.

I sail, I'll bring along "The British Colour Council Dictionary of Colour Standards," and I'll be able to beguile those dreary mid-watches by making a mental selection of colors to soak in when I get back to my room: amethyst, maroon, moss green, chestnut, flamingo.

Carveth and Moore seemed to enjoy Bob Hope's book yesterday, so I read them another installment tonight. I should have looked through it beforehand, but I didn't and suddenly I found myself in the middle of this passage: "We got our first real idea of how London has been ''it' in the blitz as we drove to the hotel. But like Bristol, and all the other British cities we saw later, life was going on as if there were no scars. The people were pretending there was nothing wrong with their city—the way you treat a friend who has some bad facial disfigurement."

My eyes were a few lines ahead of my voice, thank God!, and I was able to end the sentence at "city."

From the Plan of the Day: "Attention of all hands is called to the provisions of Alnav 48-45, which prohibits letters of condolence to next of kin of casualties for a period of 30 days after date of casualty."

April 5th. At sea

A ship is a combination firehouse, cavalry troop, and commuters' train, in that it lives and moves by gongs, bugles, and whistles. The gongs are rung only in emergencies or in homage, as when one of the high-priced hired help is coming aboard. The bugles usually supplement the whistles. But the whistles themselves—more properly, the pipes—blow all around the clock. I've never counted how many times a day the bos'n's mates pass the word, but I'd bet we never have 15 consecutive minutes without their *"Peeeeep!* Now, hear this—"

A routine day begins with *"Peeeeep!* Sunrise! Light ship!" and ends, depending on the latitude and the season, with either *"Peeeeep!* Sunset! Darken ship! The smoking-lamp is out on all weather decks!" or "Lay before the mast all eight o'clock reports!" (There are three inconsistencies in this last call, by the way: the reports aren't laid before the mast— they've brought to the exec's room; they aren't eight o'clock reports—they're ordered up almost an hour before then; and it isn't "eight o'clock"—it's "twenty hundred." But that's the Navy for you.)

Between sunrise and the end of the working day, we must hear 50 or 60 calls. They are so familiar by now that all we need is the opening phrase; the rest we can supply from memory. As soon as the pipe peeps and the bos'n's mate says, "Turn to!", we know that this will follow: "All sweepers, man your brooms! Clean sweepdown, fore and aft! Empty all trash cans and spit-kits"—delivered in a singsong cadence, with the last syllable of each phrase drawn out and falling.

Here are some of the calls we hear most often:

"All extra-duty men lay down to the master-at-arms' shack."

"General Quarters! General Quarters! All hands man your battle stations on the double!"

"Now, the smoking lamp is out throughout the ship while taking aboard aviation gasoline and fuel oil."

"Relieve the watch!"

"The break-out gang of the spud-locker detail lay down to the fantail."

"Confessions are now being heard in the crew's library."

"Now, five hands from the K division and ten hands from the fifth division report to the First Lieutenant at Number 1 crane."

"Dinner is now being served in the wardroom."

Pat Garvan told me he knew an officer of the deck who got so fed up with the whole business, he had this word passed: "Now, all those who have not done so, do so immediately!" My favorite is, "Now, the man with the key to the garbage-grinder lay below and grind same!"

Scraps: The ship had her 22,000th landing this morning, and right after it, a barrier crash—a TBM stood on its nose and knocked its propeller off, but nobody was injured.

Fashion note: One of the torpedomen wears a thin gold chain rove through the lobe of his left ear, with a gold cross hanging from the chain.

For the first few days after an attack, most of the men with topside battle stations are scrupulous about wearing helmets and carrying first-aid kits and daubing flash-proof ointment on their faces, but they get slacker and slacker as time passes, and presently they take no precautions at all. Today there was scarcely a first-aid kit to be seen on the flight deck. When the next attack comes, the cycle will repeat, but meanwhile the chaplains might preach to them on these texts:

113

"Stand forth with your helmets" and "Let thy head lack no ointment."

Bob Hope is postponed indefinitely; Carveth had to have another operation this afternoon.

April 6th. At sea

We loaded ammunition again today, so again we were outside the perimeter of the battle zone. Moreover, we got out just in time, because the other two task groups, Bull Durham (58.1) and Broncho (58.3), were worked over all afternoon —roughly, too. By 1640, when I left air plot, which was keeping score, their ships and planes had shot down 26 bogeys, and more of them still dotted the radar screen.

Even so, the attack was overshadowed by the radio news. Coop relayed it to the ready rooms in his usual majestic prose: TOKYO BROADCAST JUST ANNOUNCED THAT., THE CABNIT HAS RESIGNED. A 78 YEAR OLD., BLOKE & ALSO A RETIRED ADMIRAL HAS BEEN., GIVEN THE NOD BY HIS ROYAL PANTS.., THE RUSSIANS HAVE CALLED OFF THERE NONAGGRESS—., ION PACT WITH THE NIPS. REASON GIVEN THAT., BECAUSE THE NIPS WERE AT WAR WITH UNCLE SMA., AND THE LIMIES—TO HELL WITH IT., CAN'T RUN THIS TELETYPE ANYWAY.

April 7th. At sea

Scuttlebutt had it right for once: a Jap task group *has* stuck its nose out, and we've launched a strike to meet it —fighters, bombers, and torpedo planes, loaded with everything Ordnance could supply. At lunch, the boys were rubbing their hands: "I wish Admiral Hokipoki, or whoever he is, would head down this way, so we could get a look at 'em!"

"Me too. That *Yamato's* with 'em. they tell me, and I hear she looks like the Empire State with a foremast."

"Hell, if she's *that* big, maybe one of our BBs could hit her."

"Maybe. But she'd have to hold still. She might even—" General Quarters blew.

I was halfway up the first ladder when I realized that I had a fork in my hand. I shoved it into a pocket and kept going. A quick stop-off in flag plot to collect my windbreaker and binoculars, another stop-off at the starboard side of the bridge to snatch my helmet, hood and gloves from the overhead locker, and a final sprint to the portside speaking tube: "Flag plot, the task group dead ahead has opened fire! . . . Flag plot! . . . *Hey, flag plot!*" Their end of the tube was closed.

I ducked in to tell them, and when I got back to my station, a vast plume of smoke was rising from a carrier on the horizon to port.

"That's an oil fire," Mueck said.

To me it seemed paler than oil smoke, but it might have been faded by the haze. Jones put the long glass on it. "I can make out flames," he said. "Dunno who she is. *Essex*-class, that's all I can tell."

Mueck said, "One of the boys will know." He trotted aft to the signal bridge.

Captain Combs bellowed down from above us: "You men on the flight deck—get your steel helmets!"

Some saunterer called back, "Haven't got one, sir!"

"Well, goddam it, *get* one!"

Mueck said, "She's the *Hancock*. The fire's under control already. And a Tojo's just been splashed, 285. They didn't give me the distance." We peered out on the bearing, but we couldn't see anything.

The sheet of cloud that had covered us thinned out and blew away. We were running under a clear, limitless sky. The lookouts searched it with their glasses. Suddenly I became aware of a curious thing: utter silence had settled over the ship. For two, three, four minutes, no one on the bridge had spoken a word, nothing had come through the tube, the small noises of the flight deck had stopped completely. I wondered if I had been struck deaf. I lifted my hand to tap my ring against the compass, but hesitated, mocking myself. I listened again: the silence was still absolute. I tapped the compass. It chinked.

Jones looked at me dazedly. "Funny," he said. "I was doped off. . . ."

I started to ask him what he thought had happened, but just then the word was passed, "Flight deck crews, man flight quarter stations!" We turned into the wind, the barrier snapped up, and the ship's resumption of her rattling, thumping business drove the strange silence out of my head.

"Stand by to land aircraft!" Dick Tripp puts the white landing flag into its socket by his platform. The Fox flag is two-blocked at our yardarm.

After the F6s are down the ship turns out of the wind. The little tractors hitch onto the F6s and begin towing them aft, like ants dragging dead beetles. The whistle blows: "Set Condition One Easy in all AA batteries and material Condition Modified Afirm!" The time is 1348. We have been on the bridge about two hours.

Mueck strips off his cotton gauntlets. "Well, one more year for Germany, two more years out here, and seven years to run the Yankees out of Texas, and we can secure this goddam war!"

I hung my helmet on the speaking tube and went down to the ACI office for a cup of coffee. I had taken my first sip when GQ sounded again. Flag plot warned us, "Watch for two bogeys low on the water!"

"What's the bearing?" No answer.

The task group ahead of us started firing heavily. Their bursts made black dots on the horizon from our bows all the way around to our port quarter. They fired for five minutes, stopped, fired for another two, and stopped again. A breeze thinned the bursts and slowly erased them.

Pappy ordered, "Fighters, stand by to start engines! . . . We will catapult this flight!"

The port catapult had thrown five planes into the air (the starboard catapult was broken) when flag plot called, "Two-four-zero, 16 miles!"

Two-four-zero was approximately dead ahead. We began to come left, to bring our starboard batteries to bear. The last three fighters were launched as we were still swinging, and a spare was trundled forward and harnessed to the catapult, with its port wing folded back to clear the blast of Number 2 gun.

Jones and I smoked and ate chocolate, waiting. At 1424, the task group that was now on our starboard bow opened fire again, and presently Mueck came around the bridge with the word that two bogeys were burning on the water. The flight deck crews were already running for a view, half of them without helmets. Captain Combs's shout stopped them cold: "Myers!"

Dick Myers, the Flight Deck officer, looked up at the bridge.

"Myers, I want every man on that deck to wear a steel helmet! I've told them once today, and I'm going to hold you personally responsible! Either they wear helmets, or you put them on report!"

Dick turned up his thumb. "Aye-aye, sir!"

Most of the men fetched their helmets on the double, but there was one straggler. Pappy spotted him and blasted him

116

with the bull horn: "That man in the port catwalk, just forward of Number 2 elevator—*put on your helmet!*"

A head with a yellow hood bobbed below the deck level like a clay duck in a shooting gallery.

Another half-hour passed. A new voice came over the PA system—Joe Moody's: "Your attention, please! A flash report from one of our planes attacking the Jap fleet reports one battleship and one heavy cruiser definitely sunk!"

I was surprised that nobody cheered or even showed any excitement. I think it was because this particular enemy was so remote from us, some 300 miles away, and at the moment we were absorbed in enemies far closer. One sailor said, rather quietly, "Roger!", but that was the only response to the news.

Condition One Easy was set a few minutes later, and I went below to see Proff, who was laid up with the crud. His room is on the same deck as mine, which meant struggling to open and close the stiff gears on all those doors. I sat down, breathless, and had just lit a cigarette, when GQ sounded for the third time. Back through the doors and up the ladders . . .

None of the ships had opened fire, but CIC reported that a bogey or two was skulking around. The afternoon dragged on. A purple cloud spread over the whole west. Its southern end touched the horizon, but its tattered northern end hung clear, like a lopsided curtain. As the sun sank, it shone through a rift and flecked the purple sea with gold. No doubt Tennyson could have risen to a superb simile, but all it reminded me of was the stuff they smeared on my legs at Pearl, when I had one of those fungus rashes—Castellani's paint, I think they call it.

Mueck brought word that a bogey had been shot down only ten miles away. Evidently it didn't flame, because none of us could spot it. Secure blew. What a hell of a day!—three GQs, and we never fired a single round. It's the standing by, taut, that puts you through the wringer. Hendy capped my gloom by telling me, "Better sleep in your clothes tonight. I've got an idea the Betties will be out."

At supper, everybody was too tired to talk; I didn't get the story of the Jap task force until afterwards, from the ACI office. Several air groups took part in the attack, so it's impossible to state precisely who did precisely what. But the *Yamato* exploded and sank, and an *Agano*-class cruiser (light, not heavy) exploded and sank, and a *Takanami*-class destroyer probably sank; and even if Air Group 9's boys didn't actually sink them, they certainly didn't help them any. This was their score: Torpedo 9 put five fish into the *Yamato* and five more into the cruiser; Bombing 9 gave the cruiser either seven or eight 1000-pounders and five 500-pounders; and although the destroyer didn't get but one 500-pounder, she was burning fiercely when the strike started home.

Our losses were one SB2C, piloted by Harry Worley, with Earl Ward in the rear seat. A dozen men saw the AA hit them and watched them plunge in, just off the bow of an unidentified destroyer. Some say the plane was out of control; others swear that Worley was trying a suicide crash, but died before he could bring it off.

The fighters always have the best view of an attack, so I stopped by their ready room. They were making their strafing runs all over again, with swooping hands and droning noises. One of them was saying, "It was a hell of a sight, pals, one hell of a sight!—especially when the torpeckers bored in to make their drops. I thought, 'Jesus, they'll never get through that AA! It's murder!' And then I thought, 'Jesus, there go those poor bastards, risking their lives to drop their fish, and the goddam things won't run a hundred yards, because I've drunk all the alcohol out of 'em! Jesus!" He sat down, shaking his head.

(Later: AG 9 has a victory song: "Yamato Been a Beautiful BB, but BB, You Should See Yourself Now!"

April 8th (Sunday). At sea

0930. GQ, but the bogey proved friendly. I'd slept through breakfast, so I ventured down to the bake shop, on the third deck, after balancing my hunger against the extra ladder to climb and the extra sprint if GQ sounded again. The coffee was hot and strong, and the apple pie was hot and fresh—not only that, but Drum and Volk broke out a can of ground cinnamon for the pie. Soon, I didn't really care whether the Japs laid off or not.

They did, until after lunch, when we went to Air Defense and watched TG 58.3 blasting away at what CIC reported as two bogeys. Their bursts crept in our direction, but nobody seemed alarmed. We weren't called to GQ and three flight deck crewmen continued to scuffle and snatch one another's caps, as carefree as puppies. The only time our task group fired was just before we secured: the *Hazelwood* unloaded one round through the muzzle.

Proff came up with a really juicy piece of scuttlebutt today: On the 13th, we sail for Pearl and 10 days' availability, to repair storm and battle damage. (Time out for a query: Since "availability," in the Navy sense, is equivalent to "laid up" and therefore to "useless," why isn't it a self-contradiction? Available to whom—the shipyard workers? It's like "secure," which the Navy has also distorted to the opposite of its familiar meaning. When a ship is secured from general quarters, the doors and hatches and scuttles are not closed, made secure—they're opened. I don't get it.)

I passed Proff's word along to the Senior Medical officer, Commander Smith, and asked if he thought it had any foundation. He said, "I doubt it. Not that it wouldn't be a good idea—we've got men aboard who've hardly been off the ship for 21 months—but my guess is that we won't see Pearl before July, or June at the earliest."

So much for that.

April 9th. At sea

A quiet morning until 1215, when they blew Air Defense. Running up the ladder to the gallery deck, I lost a shoe. It clipped Rudy Rudnicki behind me, fell through the ladder, and was retrieved by Nick Cline, thank the Lord! I'd never have been able to breast the stampede and fetch it. The bogey, if any, didn't close, but presently an *Enterprise* TBM landed, bringing Capt. Walter F. Boone to relieve Captain Combs, who is being ordered to COMSEVENTHFLEET as Chief of Staff. There was a minimum of ceremony about Captain Boone's arrival. Captain Combs, Commander James, and Commander Evans were on the flight deck to meet him, and when he crawled out of the TBM's tunnel, a photographer popped a few flash bulbs, but that was all. Five minutes after the word got around that he was aboard, the sailors were referring to him as "Dan'l."

Del Paine left for home today, and I was afraid I'd have no more company during those long GQs at night, but it turned out that Captain Boone's plane also brought Comdr. Harry Davison, the head of ACI in the Pacific. He's making the rounds of the carriers and expects to be with us a couple of weeks or more, most of which he wants to spend on the bridge. His bag of news was mixed: reliefs were on the way for Pat Garvan and Bob Doyle, to their delight; to everyone's sorrow, though, he told us that Sheldon Prentice had been killed on the *Wasp*, and Frank Crowley and Maury Quint on the *Franklin*. (Captain Combs's original relief, Capt. Arnold J. Isbell, was also killed on the *Franklin*.)

119

Harry described the *Enterprise* as going to GQ at 0500 and staying at battle stations all day long; K-rations for lunch; no water in the scuttlebutts; and the heads opened only for short periods. It sounds rugged, but he said that the men were keen about it.

I felt dopey this afternoon and worse after dinner—fever, and that old drag between the shoulders that usually means another bout of malaria. Commander Smith gave me some pills and two ounces of whisky and sent me to bed. In the hope of 12 hours' sleep uninterrupted by bogeys from Kyushu, I take my text from Isaiah XXIII, 2: "Be still, ye inhabitants of the isle."

April 10th. At sea

Everything's copasetic again. Fever all gone, and I feel like taking on Joe Louis or even Commander Jackson. We fueled in the morning—Bill Ogdon left for Guam on the tanker—and loaded ammo in the afternoon. George Wright watched it with me for awhile, then we drifted down to his room and into a gum-beat.

I once knew a parson who had gone into the ministry from second base in a Class-B league, but George went there from a job as headwaiter and master of ceremonies in a Chicago roadhouse. He said, "You'll think I'm kidding, but my hitch as an m.c. was an invaluable preparation for the Navy—announcing fights, running smokers, stuff like that."

Before the roadhouse, he managed a catering business and sold Fords as a sideline. Before that, he worked in a night club at Napierville, Indiana; he owned the coatroom concession, played the E-flat alto sax in the band, and handled the sandwich table, where "we cut the bread and the cream." Before that, he was fired from college for pasting a professor. Before that—anyhow, his knockabout life has certainly left no marks on his face. He's 31, but he looks like an impish cherub.

He told me, "I'd been considering the church all this time. No, I guess I wasn't considering it so much as fighting it. At college I took all the Bible I could get and sang in the choir, but instead of going the whole way, I compromised on a premed course. Medicine is a form of service, and I conned myself into believing it was the form I wanted. Pretty soon, though, I realized that my mother had dedicated one of her boys to the Lord's work, and since I was her only son—"

120

He was ordained in 1941 and became pastor of three Evangelical churches in Paradise Parish at Mt. Pleasant, Pennsylvania. (As far as he knews, he is the only Evangelical chaplain in the Navy.) On December 7, he was sitting by his radio when he heard the news of Pearl Harbor, and he swears he actually shouted, "They can't do that to us!"

He was married and had a young son, but he applied for enlistment at once.

April 11th. At sea

From the Plan of the Day: "It is fully realized that our present operations have been tiring and difficult, but let's not lose our sense of proportion. While we may be tired, the Jap is damn miserable, and that is the way we must keep him. WE CAN'T AFFORD TO LET HIM GET A SECOND BREATH!"

The crew had just been sent to noon chow, and Hendy and I were having coffee in the wardroom, when we heard this announcement: "Secure the chow line and report to General Quarters stations!"

By the time I reached the flight deck, Air Defense was sounding, and GQ went as I made the bridge. The word: bogey 16 miles, closing. But presently Mueck came around the corner with his thumb turned down, "They got him," and in a minute or two the bull horn reported, "The bogey, a Kate, closed to within 5 miles, then opened with a Ripper CAP in pursuit. The bogey was splashed at 45 miles."

Early this morning, Pat Garvan had shown me Coop's first thought for the day: ALL READY ROOMS: ALERT YANKEES!! TODAY IS XXXXXXPPOMATTOX DAY REPEAT APPOMATTOX DAY. LET US EVERY KEEP IN MIND THE EVENTS OF THAT SUCCESSFUL CAMPAIGN WHEN THE FLAG OF JEFF DAVIS WAS STOMPED IN THE DUST. WE MUST CONTINUE TO PRACTICE THE TACTICS AND TEACHINGS OF THAT GREAT GENERAL SHERMAN WHO GUIDED SO SUCCESSFULLY THE MARCH TO THE SEA. THE FAULTERING MOVEMENTS EMPLOYED AT GETTYESBURG HAVE NO PLACE IN THIS WAR.

So, on the way to lunch, I stopped by air plot to protest Coop's partisanship. He wasn't there, but someone had posted a sign above the sofa: "Lt. Cdr. Bright spun in here from a very low altitude."

We had just finished lunch when Air Defense sounded again

and, almost in the same breath, GQ. The bridge was cold and windy now; I got my pea jacket and was latching it up when the band began to play. A Jill drove in from our starboard quarter, almost at water level, crossed our wake about 200 yards astern, ducked past a light cruiser and a destroyer which fired at it with all guns, and swerved as if to make a run on us. Instead, it straightened out again, still at water level, and crashed onto the *Missouri's* main deck, just below her forward stack.

Joe Hurley yelled, "My God! Right in one of the 20-millimeter batteries!"

The burst of flame was surprisingly small and was soon extinguished; if this *kamikaze* was carrying a bomb, it must have not exploded. My glasses brought the *Mo* almost into my lap, but she was up-sun, and I couldn't see the damage. Time, 1442.

(Later: She informed us, NO CASUALTIES X DAMAGE REPAIRED WITH PAINTBRUSH X PILOTS BODY LANDED ABOARD AND WILL BE BURIED TOMORROW WITH APPROPRIATE CEREMONIES.)

I didn't have much time to look—

1446. The guns opened up again, at another plane off to starboard, out of sight, and shot it down at 1800 yards, still out of sight. Mueck was telling me about it, when a seagull made a perfect approach up the grove and lit on the flight deck, without so much as a flap of Dick Tripp's flags. It walked around a bit then flew to the bow, perched again, ran a few steps, and shook off. One of the signalmen called, "Two-block Fox!"

Sunset tonight was out of Turner. A warm salmon light bathed the ships and flecked the seas. It was magnificent until a hack cartoonist rearranged things, poking a jagged hole in a cloud and pulling it across the sun so that its rays fanned out like a Japanese flag.

1853. Third attack, a twin-engine plane this time. I couldn't make out its type. Our fighters must have jumped it because it was a blob of flame when I first saw it, and I had only a glimpse before our guns started to slam, and the smoke from our forward turrets, firing toward our port quarter, blinded me. When my eyes cleared, the plane was down, much closer than I had expected it. It floated for about three minutes, burning brilliantly. Damn that smoke! This was the very first attack since March 18th that had come in on our port side. I could have watched it the whole way.

Mueck uncrossed his fingers. "We're OK now." But we

weren't. The task group opened fire again, and our own 5-inchers kept at it. When they finally knocked off, I thought I had a carillon between my ears.

2050. Secure from GQ. While I was stowing my pea jacket under the desk in flag plot, the Admiral called Captain Boone on the squawk-box: "How'd you enjoy your welcome today?"

Captain Boone said, "Well, I'll tell you. I'm like the old Southern mammy who used to say, 'When I sits down and begins to worry, I just falls asleep!' "

The chief topic at supper was the Jill: had it banged straight into the *Missouri*, or had it skipped off the water? Everyone else swore it skipped, but I'd have seen the spray. I was too beat up to argue. I stumbled down to my sack and fell in.

2135. Air Defense. a flare was burning off to port. I reported it through the speaking tube, and Stew Lindsay asked, "How far away?"

How far away is a light at night! I snapped at him, "I can't tell, for Christ's sake!" And right there, of course, I realized that all the Admiral wanted to know was whether it was close enough to silhouette us sharply. I called Stew to apologize, but somebody else was manning the tube.

2343. Secure, at last! Nine planes were splashed around the task group today—no, eight splashed, one crashed (the *Missouri's*. How much longer will the *Yorktown's* luck hold out? These *kamikazes* are definitely unlovable. . . .

On the way to my room, I stopped by CIC. It looked like a brokerage house at the end of a 5,000,000-share day. Half the men were wearing headsets and making plots on the big plexiglas boards, writing from behind, mirror-fashion. Others were crouched over hooded scopes. Still others were just sitting, dazed and glazed. I felt the same way. I flopped on my sack without even kicking off my shoes.

April 12th. At sea

—Which was just as well, because I'd been asleep only 40 minutes when GQ cut loose, at 0145. More flares. Those damn things make me queasy! They're treacherous, because their beauty dazzles you to the fact that you're being lined up for a torpedo attack. But the flares burnt out, and nothing developed. We were running with the wind, so the bridge was quiet and warm. Again I had the curious illusion that the ship was motionless, and I could assure myself that we were making knots only by watching a constellation alternately blotted and revealed by the navigating bridge, as we zigzagged.

0210. Secure. Flag plot says that one of our night fighters shot down the bogey, a Mavis.

0455. The Admiral's orderly on the phone: "The Admiral told me to turn you out, sir, and for you to report to the bridge." We were warned last night that we'd probably catch an all-out attack today, but flag plot had no bogeys on the screen. In fact, the only excitement before breakfast was when our dawn CAP landed. One of the planes backfired as it taxied up the deck, and every man on flag bridge jumped out of his socks. That's what three hours' sleep does for you.

The early afternoon was a tourist's dream: hot sun, no wind, and not enough clouds to make a pair of earplugs. Hendy, Jim Smith, Harry Davison, and I sat on the "verandah" —the forward end of flag bridge—and smoked and talked until 1500, when Bob Doyle popped out to warn us that a big raid was on the way down from Kyushu and was now only 80 miles away. We were steaming on 020, launching, so the gap was closing fast, but as soon as 12 fighters were in the air, we reversed course. Presently we're told that our pickets have just shot down three of the enemy, 50 miles out. It won't be long now!

Surprise! At 1540, "Set Condition One Easy, materiel Condition Modified Afirm." It seems there were two flights coming in; our patrols destroyed the first, and the second was friendly.

Down on the flight deck, a sailor was painting silhouettes of the *Yamato* and *Agano* on AG9's scoreboard. Nearby a strange group was posing for a photograph: a sailor made up as Hitler was being gripped by another sailor in flight clothes, while a third—a flight-deck chief—held a knife at his throat.

And the scuttlebutt at supper was that Germany had surrendered. GQ broke up the discussion. Many flares were burning, and the task group to starboard was firing heavily, but nobody bothered us. Secured at 2210, limp with this off-again, on-again fever.

Tomorrow is Friday the 13th.

April 13th. At sea

The Japanese Sandman dumped a truckload on me last night. When I reported to the bridge after breakfast, I learned that Air Defense had sounded at 0200. I never heard it at all—the first call, as far as I know, that I've slept through since I came aboard. What finally woke me, at 0730, was Captain Combs's voice on the PA system: "Your attention, please.

Word has just been received that President Roosevelt died today of a cerebral hemorrhage."

However, his death doesn't seem to satisfy the jinx of Friday the 13th, because the word in flag plot is that the fueling scheduled for tomorrow has been postponed. If our men—particularly the gun crews—aren't allowed to sleep the clock around pretty soon, some of them will crack. Les Brown, the Senior Dental officer, told me the other day that during the Tokyo operation, which everyone expected to be brutally rugged, the men below decks were perfectly calm. But now, six weeks later, they are so exhausted that as soon as they hear the guns open up, they turn gray and dive under tables. Les said he had been taking pulses during attacks and had found them running as high as 125. Doc Lenhardt backed him up; he says that after a big day, he has a block-long line of men at the dispensary, asking for sedatives.

2100. Air Defense, but a quick secure. Bob Lawrence came down after the first watch and said that the sky was full of bogeys; none close or closing, though.

Scraps: We topped off destroyers in the morning. The *Mertz*, I noticed, has a six-pointed star painted just below her waterline, about amidships. Nobody on the bridge had ever seen one there before and nobody knew its signficance. Before we could get a signalman to ask her about it, she stood away.

An unusually dirty ocean today, covered with oil and debris —crates, tin cans, and 5-inch shell cases, probably discarded by the carrier ahead of us. *We* don't throw tin cans over the side until we've punched their bottoms out and flattened them.

On December 7, 1944, more than eighteen weeks ago, DCNO Air ordered me to escort a party of civilians from New York to Panama City, Florida, for the christening of the Liberty ship *Wendell L. Wilkie*. This afternoon my authorization for the trip arrived from BuPers. Suppose it had been marked, "Not approved"; what then? I guess they'd call the ship back and rechristen her for some deserving Democrat.

April 14th. At sea

A new man today, after 10 hours' sleep. Throughout the task group, flags are at half-mast for Mr. Roosevelt, and will stay there for 29 days more. No black armbands, though; they're peacetime only.

1320. Air Defense. Bob Doyle called over the speaking tube that our CAP has just splashed two Betties and a Zeke, and—GQ sounded; I had to call him back. By now the CAP had splashed another Betty, Bob said. "Two raids coming in, one from northeast, other from northwest. The nearer is about 50 miles."

A few minutes later he called again. "Forty-five miles, that nearer raid. And a periscope has been sighted."

"Can you give the bearing?"

"Just a sec. . . . The *Guam* sighted it: 080, about 3,000 yards."

We had begun to turn away as I set the alidade on the bearing. We looked up and down the line, but we could see nothing.

Another call from Bob. "Three Betties tallyhoed, 060, 40 miles. Plunger base is under attack."

A cloud of smoke began to expand on the horizon. I took the bearing and reported it to flag plot: "Smoke, 320."

Flag plot said, "Don't know what it is. Plunger base bears 350."

Mueck was glummer than ever. "We're gonna have to do some shooting in a minute."

I thought so too. For diversion, I watched a destroyer crisscrossing on our port quarter, trying to sniff out the sub. Dave Nelson joined me; almost at once he pointed to some specks in the sky, high up and far out on our port beam. I polished the lenses of my binoculars, to give myself time to steady down. Mueck and Dave leaned toward me, waiting. The planes were eight Corsairs, thank God! Almost as soon as I announced it, the squawk-box spoke: "With the exception of the gunnery department, set Condition One Easy, materiel Condition Modified Afirm."

(Later: Two of three Betties shot down by our CAP were carrying so-called *baka* bombs—big, mean bastards with 18-foot wings. This is their first appearance, as far as I know, and they don't seem to be too successful. Six of them were dropped on a crippled destroyer, but only one hit it. However, that one sank it. Bill Kluss says that *baka* means "fool" in Japanese, but he doesn't know why the bombs were given such a name. I asked how he happened to be aware of it, but he ain't talking.)

1902. Air Defense again. The clear sky was as brilliantly tinted as in those desert-sunset postcards from Cairo. The

126

new moon looked like an *oeil-de-boeuf* over which the thin shade had not quite been drawn. South of it was Orion; and to the north, close by, the Pleiades. I was trying to count them through my glasses when flag plot called, "Bogey! 010, distance 25," and on the bearing a new star appeared, red and swelling. I reported, "They've got him! Stand by!" It glided down, flared, and was extinguished. "In the drink!"

The flight deck's cheers died away. There was no sound on the bridge except the tarpaulin on the Admiral's transom, which the light breeze rippled with a soft-shoe rhythm: *pat-a-pat, pat-a-pat.* The task group on 030—don't know which it is—suddenly began to flicker and sparkle, but the noise of the firing didn't reach us. GQ rang. A set of six flares was dropped on our port beam, and three other sets dead ahead. Flag plot warned us, "Bogey at 000, 15 miles, closing . . . now at 030 . . . plot has merged . . . now at 040, 25 miles . . . 055, 30 miles . . . night fighter has lost contact. . . . Stand by to secure."

We secured at 2110, and I went down to the brig with Bill Kluss, for a look at three Jap flyers who had been picked out of the drink early this morning by the destroyer *Melvin*. A Marine guard admitted us. The prisoners were in separate cells. When they spotted our collar insignia, they stood up, and I saw that all three were young and quite small. One, an ensign, had a slight wound in his cheek; the others, enlisted men, seemed unharmed. Bill interrogated them in Japanese, but the ensign could read and write a bit of English, because the guard showed me a pad which he had been using for an interrogation of his own.

He had written, "My name Richard. I am Marine. Why you fight us?"

The answer, in a laborious hand, was as despondent as it was evasive: "I no win."

On the next page the guard had written, "You know B29?"

The Jap ensign had sketched one extremely well; its characteristic tail was especially accurate. The bomb bay was open, and bombs were falling. His caption was, "Tokyo burn." Also on this page was a sketch of a Pete, a Jap floatplane. "He says he flew 'em," the guard explained.

He had written on the third page, "We treat you good," but the ensign had not made a comment.

I told Bill about the Pete. He said, "That's right. They took off from Formosa last night to scout us, and a night fighter shot 'em down just after midnight. The ensign wasn't piloting, by the way; he was just an observer. They didn't have a raft, but their life belts kept 'em afloat until the *Melvin* found 'em this morning. They didn't want to be picked up; she had to drag 'em in."

"How were they in general?" I asked. "Surly or chatty or what?"

"More ashamed of themselves than anything else. They consider it a disgrace to be captured, you know. They say they can never go home again, after the war. They don't even want me to have their families notified that they're alive."

April 15th (Sunday). At sea

An unusually gentle wakening this morning, by two bells, followed by church call. Montaigne used to have himself wakened by a string quartet. Failing that, two bells and church call will do beautifully.

The service was billed as a memorial to President Roosevelt, but George Wright didn't mention his name, although he had a natural tie-in with a poem he read: S. Hall Young's "Let Me Die." George prefaced it by saying that Young had completed three stanzas but had died suddenly, just after starting the fourth—a perfect parallel to Roosevelt's three-and-a-butt terms. Jack Kitchen, Fighting 9's skipper, read the scripture. It began, "Let us now praise famous men," so it made me think of Kipling's "A School Song," which begins with that line and goes on, appropriately enough,

> *Each degree of Latitude,*
> *Strung about Creation*
> *Seeth one or more of us . . .*
> *Keen in his vocation.*

While we were fueling this afternoon, the three prisoners we saw last night were transferred to the tanker, and a destroyer put another prisoner aboard, in a stretcher. His scalp and face were a raw, purplish brown—evidently a burn—and the flesh around his eyes was so swollen that he couldn't open them. Two Marines with pistols escorted the stretcher down to sick bay, but the ship's cat, if we had one, could have handled this poor devil.

0040. Air Defense, then—as usual—GQ as I made the bridge. A bogey at 000 to within 5 miles, but turned tail. Another was reported at 340, 40 miles. Whatever task group is on that bearing stopped firing after a few rounds. Secured at 0110 except the Gunnery Department, which was kept alert for another 20 minutes.

0430. Air Defense again, but no GQ and no firing. A warm, calm night, with the stars lower on the horizon than I've ever seen them before. Our task group suddenly entered a broad patch of phosphorus, and the wakes of the nearer ships became brilliant, although it was still too dark to distinguish the ships themselves. Secured at 0515, just as the east was turning red, and I was turning gray.

0810. Air Defense *again!* On my way topside, a talker told me that no bogeys were closing, so I stopped by air plot to leave a magazine for Carl Ballinger. Pete Joers was there, doing his imitation of a *baka* bomb, in which he looks exactly like an orbiting turkey buzzard.

The first sweep was already taking off. You watch a fighter scud past beneath you, but when it reaches the catapults, or thereabout, your eyes drop it and pick up the next one; almost never do you follow a fighter into the air. You watch a bomber or a torpecker the same way, but with this difference: after you drop it and pick up the next, you always turn back for a glance at the first one. This morning I think I've discovered the explanation: when a TBM or an SB2C crosses the ramp, the deck no longer doubles the roar of its engine. The suddenly diminished volume of noise registers subconsciously, and you glance to make sure that the plane is airborne.

When the last was gone, two fighters were spotted on the catapults, but orders were changed, and a tractor looked onto the starboard plane and began towing it aft. All at once Captain Combs's voice blasted down from the navigating bridge: "Stop, goddamit! *Stop!*"

Too late. The starboard wing tip smashed into Number 1 turret and crumpled. Before the skipper drew breath, I had gained a new appreciation of Job's line, "the thunder of the captains, and the shouting." The plane, by the way, was Number 13.

After "Secure," I bummed a cup of coffee from Pat Garvan

in the ACI office. Its decorations now include a hangman's noose, with this placard attached:

JOERS: TAKE NOTE—
KEEP THE HELL OUT!
(signed) ZORRO Z.

Pat and Pete are roommates, so it's probably one of those *when*-are-you-going-to-put-out-that-goddam-light feuds.

I had only three hours' sleep last night; and it turned out, at noon chow, that Pat Patterson hadn't been able to get any at all. Both of us were shoveling in the last spoonful of ice cream, and bragging how we were going to pound our mattresses this afternoon—"Mine'll be so flat, it won't have but one side," Pat said—when *clang! clang! clang!*

Several bogeys were in the air, but CIC reported that none was close, so everyone on flag bridge relaxed. Right then it happened. The ships directly ahead open fire together, and a plane crashes on the rim of the formation. A moment later, another crashes just off the *Missouri's* stern; its bomb blows a column of brown water higher than her foretop. A third plane crashes next door, alongside the destroyer *McDermut*. I don't think it hit her, but white smoke is pouring from her stack. The whole task group is firing now. The *Intrepid* takes one! Her flight deck seems to be afire, although I know I saw spray shoot up from her bow. The Jap must have bombed her, then crashed in. We make an emergency turn to port; the *Intrepid's* losing station and falling astern. Now smoke is coming from her hangar deck too. I hope to God she can control her fires!

Half an hour has passed. She's holding her new station. Her hangar deck is still gushing smoke, but it's paler than before, so the flames haven't reached her av-gas.

Another half hour. She's now about 3,000 yards on our port beam. She's smoking hardly at all, and aside from a slight list to port, she's showing no damage. Her flight deck is evidently usable, because all but half a dozen of the planes that were spotted aft have been towed forward. There's a cluster of men at the forward end of her island, but otherwise things seem normal.

Poor 'Dry I!' Lucky *Yorktown!*

(Later: The attack began at 1320 and lasted 15 minutes. Two planes, not one, dove on the *Intrepid* simultaneously. She shot down one close aboard her starboard bow, but the other hit the port side of her flight deck, aft, ripping a 12 by 14 foot hole, destroying 40 planes, and killing nine men and wounding 40, six of them seriously. The *McDermut* wasn't damaged by the Jap, but by a 5-inch shell of the *Missouri's*, which plugged her just above the waterline; two dead, seven injured.)

During the first furious minutes, the unoccupied men on the flight deck rushed from side to side for a better view. If a bomb or *kamikaze* had hit us then, it would have been like hitting the bleachers at a World Series game. Pappy Harshman lashed them with the bull horn, but excitement had made them deaf. They hadn't dispersed until we began landing 13 F6's from CAP 3. As the last came up the groove, Pappy announced, "The next plane will make landing Number 23,000," and a very pretty landing it was.

(Later: We passed another milestone in the last attack: Number 2 5-inch fired its 1,000th round, and my friends in the bakeshop, Drum and Volk, presented the gun crew with a huge square cake, its corners fortified with pink miniature twin mounts.)

Three belly tanks have just drifted past. One is much darker than the others; wonder if it's Japanese? Mueck says he saw a drifting torpedo this morning.

April 17th. At sea

0817. General Quarters again: the fourth—or is it the fifth?—since yesterday afternoon. There seems to be a big aerial melée up north. Bob Doyle tells us the three large groups of enemy planes have broken through our patrols and are closing us fast; in fact, they're less than 30 miles away right now. I smeared my face with flash paint and turned the big signal searchlight inboard to see if I'd left any gaps. O my God! Fox 13 has been repaired and is spotted directly below us! But even as I crossed my fingers, it taxied forward and was catapulted.

Skip Brown called through the tube, "Raid still closing. . . . Stand by a minute! Splash two Betties!"

"Thanks. Any other word?"

"I'll say! A large number of"—it sounded like *turbulence*—"very low, coming in"—*very fast?* His excitement blurred his words so that I couldn't catch them. I told him, "Please say again!" and pressed my ear against the tube.

It still sounded like *turbulence*. Skip asked, "Did you get it this time?"

The anxious signalmen hung on my answer. "Sorry, I couldn't get it at all."

Skip said, "I'll send the word out to you by Henderson." And Hendy, wearing full war paint and all his battle gear and a tremendous grin, came out with a slip of paper on which he had written, "Large number flabbit turglums very low coming in cadzer freeth."

The double-talking stinker!

I told the signalmen, "My former friend Mr. Henderson, here, lives in San Mateo, California. I know his street address, and the minute this war's over, we'll all meet in front of his house and draw straws for the pleasure of cutting his black heart out. OK?"

Skip interrupted with another message: "The raid has clarified: 24 planes coming in from the north."

"Is this one on the level?"

"Absolutely!—Whoa! Correction! I see there's a dash between the 2 and the 4. Two to four planes coming in."

As he spoke, the task group to the north opened fire. A red flame broke out thousands of feet in the air and plunged into the sea. The Jap must have been in a power dive when he was killed. The firing continued. Despite it, we began to land our patrol. The forth F6 overshot, and its tail hook didn't catch quite soon enough. Its prop ticked Number 3 barrier with a clear, sweet *ting!*

Just then, the word was passed, "Bogey 050, 25, closing." We waved off the rest of the patrol and came to a course of 210, which brought us from under the scattered clouds.

Bob Doyle stuck his head out from flag plot. "One of the pilots that just landed says they had a hell of a fight. He shot down six Japs himself, and the guys in his section shot down a lot more, but about 20 others got away."

(Later: It turned out to be Gene Valencia's section. Gene splashed six plus two probables, Jim French and Harris Mitchell splashed three apiece, and Clint Smith splashed two. This division ran up a score of 50 Jap planes before its tour was over.)

1030. CIC reported, "Screen is Clara." We reversed course to resume landing the patrol, and I went below for coffee, having missed breakfast. The *Missouri* has sent us a series of photos of the *kamikaze* that crashed her on the 11th (I was right: it didn't skip off the water; it hit her full on), so I took them up to show Captain Combs. When he came to the Jap pilot's burial with honors, he said, "Well, I suppose that's the decent thing to do, but I'd rather handle it the way the

132

Intrepid did yesterday. She sent us a dispatch saying, 'Have thrown pilot's remains over the side.' "

As the poet says, "To be tender-minded does not become a sword."

1105. Air Defense. Pat Garvan stopped off at flag bridge on his way from the pilothouse. "Take it easy," he said. "Today is SP-plus-M, so nothing's going to happen to us."

"SP-plus-M?"

"Sure: one month after St. Patrick's Day."

Captain Boone also stopped, on his way topside. "How about that boy who just shot down six Japs? It wasn't so long ago that stuff like that was getting the Congressional Medal!"

Nobody seems to have any word on the approaching bogeys—how many, what bearing, how far. We were running through the standard comparisons for CIC's fat-dumb-and-happiness when Pappy Harshman told the flight deck, "Target CAP 5 and CAP 3 prepare to start engines!" I'm sure that each of us completed the familiar series, silently, to himself: "Stand clear of propellers! . . . Start engines!" I know that I did, and I know that in this confusion and uncertainty, the small routine was a comfort.

Proff came down from the pilothouse for a smoke. He says that when we fuel tomorrow, we get the *Randolph* as an additional replacement (the *Independence* has already joined up) for the *Intrepid*, which has been sent home for repairs. Lord knows we can use the *Randolph!* Of the eleven CV's that started this operation with our task force, only six are left.

Proff and I were reminiscing about Australia, as usual, when we noticed that the AA crews were putting on their helmets and standing to their guns. Sometimes they get the word before flag bridge does. Proff jumped for the ladder, and I was buckling my own helmet, when the squawk-box uttered another of its preposterous, infuriating trivialities: "Now, the movie operator dial 222!"

Around 1300, the *Remey* came alongside to top off. Two Scotties were frisking on her deck. They weren't wearing life preservers, although I should think they'd need them more than would the *Washington's* dog.

Presently we have a pet of our own. A bird hovering over the forward ramp drifted a little too far aft, and the slipstream of a TBM turning up on the port catapult hurled him down the deck in wild wingovers. He came out of it like a veteran stunt pilot—shoved his stick forward, kicked left rudder, and made a smooth two-point landing on Number 2 elevator. I put my glasses on him. He was about the size and build of a thrush, and was speckled like a hen quail, except for some yellow stripes on his breast. We were 85 miles from land—Okinawa—at the moment, but I'd swear that this was a land bird. He strutted around a few minutes, then took off.

1430. Air Defense and GQ. "Bogey, 120, 9 miles." Only nine miles again! CIC is cutting its warning shorter and shorter. I saw a splash on the horizon, but it wasn't the kind that a plane makes, and it was 30° north of the reported bearing. We waited for further word, but all we got was another of those damned announcements: "The *Guam* will unload one gun through the muzzle."

Flash! Boom! A black puff. "Set Condition One Easy!"

On my way to the Operations office, where some work had piled up for me, all the talk I overheard was about the wonderful job our patrols have done today, so I went to ACI for the figures.

I started work at 1450. . . . The next thing I knew, it was 1730. A paper clip was stuck to my cheek, where it had rested on the desk, and my left leg was still asleep. If GQ had sounded, I'd have had to *crawl* up the three ladders to the bridge. I still have 200 pages of bulletins and memoranda to absorb before I can turn in, thanks to my nap. I'm glad I had it, though, seeing Pat Patterson at supper. The poor devil is really beat up. He's usually nimble with a knife and fork, but tonight he just stared at his food, then shoved the plate away and put his head on the table and went to sleep.

Later: Here's the explanation of our last GQ. At 1425, the second section of our RAPCAP—four fighters, led by Don Graham—was vectored onto a bogey at 16,000 feet, 40 miles from the task group. The Jap plane, a Frances, at once dived to 500 feet, with the Hellcats on its tail, and when they finally caught up, it was only seven miles from its target. Don had first crack, but nothing happened; his barrels, he discovered, had been burnt out in the fight this morning; so he stood aside and took gun-camera shots of Toby Larson making the kill.

April 18th. At sea

Slept until 0800 without a single GQ or Air Defense. Bob Lawrence says the reason we drew a bye is that the B29's worked over the Kyushu airfields last night and flattened some Jap plans as well as planes. Paul Brogan bears him out.

He was down at the brig when the word was passed to secure, and one of the Jap prisoners yelled, "My God, don't secure *now!* There's a big raid scheduled!"

Tom Stetson, VT9's skipper, has promised to let me go on their Okinawa strike this afternoon, and Clyde Lee has offered me a ride. At 1441 our TBM staggers into take-off position. Mugridge, the turret gunner, asks, "Got your straps on tight?"

I lean into them, straining. "Affirmative."

The flight deck runs past us. I can't feel it when Clyde picks up his wheels, but when he closes his flaps, the plane jumps forward and falls 50 feet. I throw off the safety belt and shoulder straps and wriggle into my chute harness. TBM Number 130 drifts up alongside to port, and 128 to starboard; 128 is carrying only one rocket; the rest of us have two.

Lee: "I count 13 planes joined up. Is that what you make?"

Mugridge: "Affirmative."

Thirteen! Hoping that they're wrong, that there are either 12 or 14 of us, I peer through the ports. They *are* wrong, thank God; I can't see but 11. Wait: I can see 13 shadows on the water. And this is my thirteenth mission. . . .

Our last circle takes us past the task group and gives me my first good bird's eye view of the *Yorktown* since the bomb hit her; the patch on her starboard side is like a stale bandage, rusty with blood.

1517. I can't stop yawning. The GQ nights are collecting payment. Besides, there's not enough chatter on the air today to hold anyone's interest. The Offical squawks about radio discipline seem to have taken effect. [Since making this entry, I've come to believe that yawning is not necessarily a symptom of sleepiness. Many men have told me that they were seized with fits of yawning just before action.]

1533. We climb to 4000 feet through scattered clouds. It is noticeably cooler at this altitude; not only that, but the onions I ate at lunch are beginning to nudge me. The sea has lost its up-and-down motion entirely. It looks as if someone were dragging a snug blue film across its rough surface. Still climbing: 4200, 4400, 4800 . . .

1542. Okinawa in sight. Our formation crosses at Kimmu Wan and heads south. Several destroyers are bombarding shore installations. Far below is a poky biplane; must be an SOC, spotting for a cruiser. We're spiraling down now: 3600, 3000, 2400. . . . Considerable traffic is on the roads, much more than two weeks ago. Napalm is burning everywhere, leaving ugly black holes in the green fields and red-roofed villages. The air is getting rough, maybe from the burning villages, maybe from shell bursts. Machinato airfield is ahead of us, and past it, Naha and its airfield. A sunken ship at the foot of a cliff. Two radio towers, prostrate. Still spiraling: 2000, 1500, 1200. . . . Now the vermiculations are revealed as trench systems. Craters pock the whole landscape. Not a living thing anywhere. Our plane seems barely moving, yet our shadow rushes along with reassuring speed. Tracers are prodding a village astern. Still spiraling down: 800, 600, 500. . . .

1617. Clyde straightens out for his bombing run. His wing guns begin to *pop-pop-pop-pop*, and their acrid smoke floods the bilges. The plane drags as the bomb-bay doors open. Our target is a battery of artillery concealed in a village. The bombs drop, hesitate, then point downward. They're fused for a 10-second delay, so even though we're almost skimming the ground, I've got plenty of time to crawl aft to the stinger and watch the explosion. There they go! Smoke leaps up 200 feet, carrying a dozen or 15 bodies which pinwheel slowly.

A quiet voice comes through my phones: "You Melrose plane that just dropped those bombs ["Melrose" is our new call sign]—for your information, you just killed some Japs."

We're circling again. Now I understand something that has puzzled me since my other mission. The Okinawa countryside is dotted with round, bare spots, roughly 15 yards across, each with a thick beam in the middle. I'd thought they were range finders or sites for guns, but I see now that they're simply threshing-floors.

Suddenly there's a loud *rrrrrrrip!*, and our rockets are gone. I'm searching for the target when a voice breaks in, "Hello, Melrose. This is Whisky. I've just found a park of nice, juicy trucks. If you have any bombs or ammo left, how about joining us?"

Our strike leader's answer is as eager as Gimlet's used to be: "This is Melrose 201. Wilco!"

Whisky is the air-support co-ordinator, orbiting below us in his little Cub. "Roger, Melrose," he says. "They're in target area eight-zero-seven-two. Follow me. Out."

The grid chart shows that target area 8072 is a low knob just west of Yonabaru Airfield. From my position in the bilges, I can't see us approach it, but when Clyde starts strafing, I wait a moment, then press the trigger of my .30. It fires one round and jams. They empty cartridge case is stuck over the case behind it. By the time I clear the round and reload, the target is miles astern.

1712. The TBMs are gathering. Clyde dips his nose, our

section joins up, and we head for home. I'm glad to take off my helmet; it's hot and too big for me; it kept sliding over my eyes. Mugridge and I light cigarettes and relax. Those pinwheeling bodies—they didn't "open like a beautiful rose," or however Vittorio Mussolini described his bombing of the Ethiopian tribesmen; but if they gave me no feeling of beauty, and none of heroism, they certainly gave none of savagery either. I don't feel guilt or even regret. This is an impersonal war. In your own mind, you're not killing men; you're destroying an enemy.

1801. Clyde calls, "Task group is in sight, 10 miles dead ahead. Guns on safe?"

"Affirmative." I swap the chute harness for the shoulder straps. Clyde shakes his wings as the break-off signal; the wheels go down, then the flaps. Mugridge runs through the check-off list: "Prop in low pitch?" and so on. The *Yorktown's* wake becomes tangent to our curve. Our tail hook catches, and CRASH! The extra can of .50-caliber ammo breaks loose from the bulkhead and grazes my right ankle. The can weighs about 60 pounds. My thirteenth mission. . . .

As I came out of the shower, the squawk-box announced that Ernie Pyle had been killed on Ie Shima this morning.

Scraps: Carl Ballinger announced at supper that there hadn't been a single bogey on the screen all day.

"Nude-noggin" Bright is still burning over a fresh insult from Pete Joers, who told him, "When you get home, Coop, don't go into any poolrooms. Don't even walk by the door, or somebody'll sure stick a cue in your ear!"

April 19th. At sea

Today is the anniversary of the Battle of Lexington but, for a change, this embattled farmer doesn't have to stand on the rude bridge; I've got another hop lined up.

I'd flown in an SB2C before, but only from Vero Beach to Miami; I'd never had a combat mission in one. They hadn't reached the Solomons when I left in February 1943, and the *Lexington's* dive bombers, in 1944, were SBDs. Bombing 3 flew 2Cs, of course, but the AGC had a "no hitchhikers" rule. Herbie Houck is less strict; so are his squadron commanders; and when I told Tony Schneider, Bombing 9's skipper, that Tom Stetson was letting me fly with his torpeckers, he said he'd take me along the first chance he got. This morning at breakfast he came over and whispered, "OK for the 1000 strike, if MT [the Air Officer]

137

doesn't find out. Better be at Ready 4 about an hour beforehand."

I was there. Tony said I'd be flying with Jack Bell, so after the briefing, I got Jack's regular gunner, Hays, to check me out in the rear seat. Hay's fingers flicked a dozen switches and levers: "You push this catch down and swing it like *this*, see, because it locks in only two positions, fore and aft. Here's the jack for your mike. The mike usually clips into that bracket there, but we keep it *here*. One last thing: before a crash landing, break out the raft and hold it in front of you. These 2Cs float a good while, but it's a good thing to save as much time as possible."

(Keep talking, brother! You've got a point there!)

0940. "Pilots, man your planes!" 0949. "Start engines!" A radioman stops at each plane and holds up an inquiring thumb. I hold up mine: phones OK. 1003. We get the checkered flag and sweep off the ramp smoothly—no stoop, no squat, no bump. As in SBDs, you are told to keep your canopy open on take-offs and landings, so that you can get out fast, but to close it in normal flight, to cut down wind resistance. I close mine when I hear Jack's close, at 500 feet, and begin the strap-and-harness routine. By the time I'm finished, our flight has joined up. Our plane has Number 2 position (portside) in the tail-end V. The first V is above us to port; the second, below us to port. Eleven TBMs are overhead, with two F6Fs far out on each flank. The whole formation steadies on its course to the target, climbing gently.

The rearseatman in Number 115, leading our V, is old "Snap-snap," a chief photographer's mate who has flown more missions than many of the pilots. He and the rearseatman in 103, on our starboard wing, are talking by hand-taps—fist for a dot, palm for a dash—but they're much too fast for me to eavesdrop.

A hideous fragment comes over the phone: "They're throwing everything in the book out there today!"

1034. We start a circle to starboard. The Vs cock their port wings and show that we're carrying two 250-pound wing bombs in addition to the 1000-pounder in our bays. 1042. Okinawa. The whole area where we cross the island is burning like the Valley of a Thousand Smokes. Now our strike leader calls the air-support co-ordinator: "Hello, Whisky. This is 201 Melrose. Over."

"Hello, 201 Melrose. This is Whisky. Over."

"Hello, Whisky. I have 11 Victor Tare with 1000-pound

bombs, plus four rockets on eight of the Victor Tare; I have four Victor Fox with napalm, and I have 12 Victor Baker with 1000-pounders and two 250-pounders. Over."

"Roger, Melrose 201. What are your instructions?"

"Our instructions are to leave here by 1200."

"Roger. Out."

Jack Bell points to Naha Airfield, under our starboard wing. "See that place? That used to be the hottest spot out here. The first pilot this squadron lost was right there—Mitch Bailans. If we'd had weather like this, it wouldn't have happened, but there was this thick, low overcast, and when we went down to identify our targets, the AA nailed him."

We circle the west coast for another 20 minutes before Whisky calls us: "Hello, Melrose 201. Come into the island with your flight. Watch to stay south of the line between Yonabaru and Naha." He breaks off to tell Shasta 305, "If you run into any AA on the beach, let me know, and I'll send some Victor Fox down to strafe it for you." Then back to us: "201 Melrose, split your flight and send your Victor Baker and Victor Fox to report to Hindu 3 [a sub-co-ordinator] at target area 7767, areas King, Love, Peter, Queen, Roger, Sugar, Tare, and send your Victor Tare to target area 8172. . . . Hello, Hindu 3. Your target is four enemy guns in a cave in those areas, on the main road near Yonabaru. Do you have that?"

Hindu 3 answers, "Just a minute. I'll go down and look."

I locate the target on the grid chart and finally identify it beneath us. It's a bare piece of ground, apparently about the size of a football field, bracketed on three sides by a red-roofed shed. Even as I'm looking, there are four winks of fire—the battery firing a salvo.

Whisky calls us again. There's been a foul-up; we're to change targets with the torpeckers, who had been assigned to another battery, concealed in caves cut into a notch through a hill, where a small road runs. The notch is extremely difficult to see, unless you're sighting right down it, and our bombers have a tough time keeping it in view.

Hindu 3: "I'll make a rocket run on the target and mark it for you. Stand by. . . . God damn! Overshot a little! I've got one smoke rocket left. Stand by again. . . . Bingo!"

Our fighter leader, 101 Melrose: "I saw that. Seems to be some personnel down there, so I'll put my napalm in there too."

Whisky: "Roger. Give 'em everything you've got. They

have guns in those caves. They wheel 'em out and fire 'em and wheel 'em back."

Hindu 3: "And make your run from east to west, east to west."

We're supposed to shove off for home by 1200, and it's 1145 already, but we're still climbing for bombing altitude. The hell of it is, the higher we get, the more the target blends into the terrain; worse, small clouds are beginning to drift across the area, each blanketing it for several minutes. We climb to 4300 feet, where we level off. From here the target is anybody's guess. Melrose 207 complains that he can't identify it at all.

Hindu 3: "Have you got it spotted yet?"

Melrose 207: "Request you make one more strafing run."

"Wilco. I will begin my run in 30 seconds. . . . Did you see that?"

"Negative. Too damn many planes and clouds around here."

"I am now commencing another strafing attack. Watch your target, please!"

Melrose 207 makes no comment.

1217. One by one the bombers go into their dives. Jack pushes over from 4000 feet and pulls out low enough for me to feel the bump of the explosion. Hindu 3 says, "The last Melrose plane that dropped—you were south and east." We are late at the rendezvous; the other planes are on their way home when we finally join up. Chief Snap-snap catches my eye, holds up two fingers, and points at our wing. I call Jack: "What about our wing bombs? Haven't we still got 'em?"

Jack pulls wide, drops them, and takes his place again. Off helmet, and a cigarette.

1240. There's the task group in the distance. I begin fixing my shoulder straps. Wait: this TG has three CVs, so it isn't ours. Here's another one. No, still isn't ours. But there's ours at last, and there's our little cottage with the roses 'round the door, and the big "10" on her flight deck. We circled at 2000 feet while the ships turn into the wind, scrawling 23 commas on the blueboard of the sea (wow!).

Down we go. Men are sunning themselves on the *Wisconsin's* 5-inch turrets. I hear a roar which means that Jack has opened his canopy, so I open mine. At 1313, he greases the big plane in for a perfect landing.

(Jack was killed three weeks later.)

Ready 2 showed a movie tonight—"Convoy," a British production starring Clive Brook. Officers of the Royal Navy and the German Navy evidently go into battle wearing dress blues, complete with ribbons and stiff collars. Wonder if the American public thinks *we* look like that? (said he, borrowing a safety pin to hold his khaki shirt together.)

April 20th. At sea

At supper tonight we were idly guessing ages, and everyone was surprised that Joe Moody had had his forty-first birthday two days ago. Most of us had reckoned him at least six years younger. His gentle spirit must smooth and shield his face. Every time I look at him, I think of another young priest, the priest of Aesculapius and Apollo in *The Woman of Andros,* whose serene expression made Pamphilus wish he had his life to live over again, and made Simo reflect, "People like that have some secret about living. . . . They know something that prevents their blundering about, as we do."

April 21st. At sea

0045. Air Defense and GQ.

Flag plot called through the speaking tube, "Bogey 135, 35, closing . . . 133, 30 . . . tallyho!"

The Chief of Staff came to the tube: "He's off to port. Watch for him!"

Almost at once flag plot called again, "Splash one Irving, 130, 26!" But if the Irving flamed, the low, heavy clouds in the southeast hid it.

Another bogey came over the tube: "We've got him at 025, 62, closing . . 50 . . . 40 . . . 35 . . . merged plot . . . splash one Betty!" No sign of that one, either.

0146. Secure, and back to bed, after glancing at the Plan of the Day, which ends, "We can expect another test of our strength today. We are ready. Keep alert!! Heads Up!!"

0700, in the ACI office. Pat Garvan is being detached next week with orders giving him 30 days' leave before reporting for his new duty at Jax (NAS Jacksonville).

Commander Evans: "How'd you wangle all that leave? You must know somebody, Pat. I always say, it's 90 per cent *whom* you know in the Navy, and only 10 per cent *what* you know."

Pat, pretty huffily: "You can be damn sure it's not Mr. Forrestal. My dog once chewed up his goat."

We were probing this extraordinary incident when Dave Nelson came in with word that the B-29s were about to plaster Kyushu again, after having been weathered out for two days. Lord, I hope it's true! If they do, they ought to nail down the *kamikazes* for at least another day. (Judge Allen, the other photo interpreter, calls the *Yorktown a* "kamicarrier.")

0800, in air plot. Pete Joers pointed to Coop's hairless head and remarked dreamily, "All I want to know is, how the hell did they put eyes in that stump?"

0930. Dave's good news is all over the ship. The tension has relaxed until you'd think we were pleasure-cruising in the Caribbean. One of the chiefs in air plot is playing Idiots' Delight. On the flight deck, men are lounging in the sun; in the passageways, they're scuffling happily. It's about time they had a little rest. Earlier this morning I saw a certain officer whom I hadn't run across in several days. I hardly recognized him. He has become as gray and drawn as a corpse with its throat cut.

1420. Air Defense. "Bogey 250, 22 miles." Jones came by with a later word: "It's now 240, 14 miles, angels 30 [Altitude, 30,000 feet]."

I said, "Angels *thirty?* Must be a spotter. Trouble tomorrow!"

"Or tonight," Jones said.

"Fourteen miles is too damn close. Why don't they call us to GQ?"

Just then it sounded, and just as it finished, the squawk-box yelled, "Plane closing! Plane diving on us!"

Every man on flag bridge ducked, waited, then craned at the sky. "Where? I don't see it! Where the hell is it?"

The squawk-box yelled in answer, "The *Guam* sighted it! Bogey opening, course 030! Secure from General Quarters!"

We have yet to see the plane.

From GQ we went to One Easy. The ship was still buttoned up. I couldn't get to my room, but Hendy's was fairly accessible, so I dragged myself down to his sack and an hour's nap. Air Defense brought me out of it standing up, and I made the bridge as Skip Brown called over the tube, "Four bogeys, 18 miles."

"Got a bearing for us?"

"Just a sec. . . . Sugar Baker Two Charlies," (SB2C's) and we went to One Easy again.

1800. Supper. Reggie Carey, who has just reported aboard as Pat Garvan's relief, asked what I considered the best battle station. It's hard to say. The fo'c'sle is good, but if you have to go over the side, you'll probably be run down. The fantail is fine for jumping, but bad for smoke and flames. The important thing is to remember to take the windward side; if you take the lee, the ship will bear down on you.

1850. Air Defense. A pale, pinkish-gray, dove's-breast sunset—beautiful until you realize it's on our port side; we're cruising north again. However, flag plot assures us that there's nothing on the radar screen; Air Defense was simply a precaution against a sudden dusk attack, expectable in view of this afternoon's scurry.

The Admiral came out on the bridge for a breather. We fell to talking about home, and I asked when he thought his tour would be over. "I don't know," he said. "I'd like to stay here another year, but I don't think it's fair for me to have this wonderful experience and not share it with others." One man's meat . . .

Then Bob Doyle came out, and I told him about the discussion with Reggie. Bob said, "All I know is, I'd rather have your battle station than mine. Where I am, in flag plot, the battle ports keep you from seeing anything, and even what you hear is second-hand. The only dope you get is from the phones and the squawk-box and the speaking tube—that is, until our own guns open up. The 5-inchers don't bother me; they may be firing at a bogey miles away. I begin to worry when the 40s cut in, because the bogey is that much closer. But when the little 20s start to chatter, I know the bogey is right on top of us, and that's when I *really* sweat it out. The hell of it is, it may not be diving at us at all. It may be after the ship next door. *You* can see it, here on the bridge, but *we* just sweat it out."

I said, "Sometimes we see it, but the few times bogeys have caught me in flag plot, I've felt like a blind man in a bull ring."

Exactly at that moment GQ blew, and the task group opened fire. Just enough light was left to show the bogey. It came in fast, straight at us—I thought, "A dead whale or a stove boat, Ahab!"—but broke off at the last second and ducked between us and the destroyer on our port bow. I don't know which destroyer she was, but she tracked the whole way, some of her shells bursting right in our faces.

When the firing stopped, I turned to tell Bob, "Well, that's at least one show you've been able to watch," but he'd missed it; GQ had hauled him back to his coop in flag plot.

2125. Secure, and coffee in the wardroom.

Before turning in, I stopped by Doc Lenhardt's room and asked his opinion on the question of inside vs. outside battle stations. Doc said, "Did I ever tell you about the time I was on a ship evacuating Marine casualties from Tulagi? One of my patients was in a hell of a mess, with a fractured humerus and a through-and-through wound in his throat. I fixed his throat and was getting ready to put an airplane splint on his arm, when the ship's 5-inchers began to bang, and then the 3-inchers, and then the .50-caliber machine guns, and then the little Lewis guns mounted on the boats on deck. When I heard *those* little buggers, I knew that goddam Nip plane was just about to come into sick bay with me. I thought, *We're gonna have to abandon ship here in a minute, and a guy with an airplane splint would sink like an anvil———*"

Air Defense sounded. Time, 2345. Halfway out the door, I stopped. "What happened?"

Doc was looking for his cap. "I made a quick shift and put on a cast instead."

"What happened to the ship?"

"Oh, the Nip missed us."

He found his cap and ran aft, toward the ladder to sick bay. I ran forward, toward the ladder to the hangar deck. Then I thought of something else and called to him, "How about the Marine?"

Doc's voice reached me faintly. "Next time I saw him, his arm had healed perfectly. See you later!"

After about 10 minutes, flag plot notified the bridge, "Splash one Betty, 46 miles," but we didn't secure until 0035, and the sky was still full of bogeys. On the way down to my room, it occurred to me that the men on the flight deck haven't been wearing their flashproof paint for nearly a week. I don't know whether they're getting bold or weary or plain indifferent.

The Plan of the Day had been distributed. It ends, "In the groove again, so heads up!"

April 22nd (Sunday). At sea

The first installment of sleep lasted exactly half an hour; GQ turned us out at 0115. Bill Dunn shot the breeze with me on the bridge, while one bogey closed to 40 miles and another to 20. No firing. Secured around 0200.

I booked another Okinawa mission with VB-9 today: "Support Dog," scheduled for 1445. Just as I got to Ready 3 for the briefing, the teletype clicked off, BOMBER 106 MADE CRASH LANDING AT OKINAWA X PILOT AND GUNNER RESCUED. The slate showed that Ed Wiezorek had been flying 106. We were speculating about him when the rest of his strike returned and gave us the story. They were carrying bombs with instantaneous fuses, they said, and Ed pulled out of his dive so low—around 600 feet— that he was probably caught in his own blast. One of the boys disagrees; he saw a burst of heavy AA near Ed's port wing, so it may have been a shoot-down. Anyhow, he made a nice, controlled landing on a shallow reef, and an Army ambulance drove out and picked him up. Neither he nor his gunner, Carlton Walker, was injured.

GQ goes, and here I am, buckled into my life jacket and chute harness! I shucked them off and tore along the portside catwalk, across the flight deck, and up to flag bridge. The *Alaska* was whanging away at something I couldn't see but presently the word was passed that the bogey had opened, and "We are unloading one of our guns through the muzzle."

Of the twelve 5-inchers aboard, of course it had to be one in Number 2 mount, right in our laps. We covered our ears, waited for what seemed ten minutes, then *BOOM!*, and charred flakes blew down the bridge, along with a stench of ammonia. Among the flakes was, mysteriously, a peanut. Jimmy Smith stared at it. "I always suspected it." he said. "Now I know it. Between alerts, they use that goddam gun as a scrapbasket."

"Set Condition One Easy," the squawk-box announced.

I racked my helmet, scampered back to Ready 3, and re-arrayed myself in my flight gear. GQ again! I hesitated. The pilot I was assigned to, Billy Watson, said, "The hell with it! We've got to get our show on the road. Come on!" We ran out to our plane, with the other pilots. Luck was with us; One Easy was set as we climbed aboard. I snuggled down

145

and was checking my phones when be damned if GQ didn't blow for the *third* time!

Our bomber was spotted in the tail-end Charlie position; we couldn't get air-borne for 15 minutes. Meanwhile, out there on the naked deck, with no protection except two small sheets of armor plate, and squatting on the edge of the after ramp, where the least puff from a bomb would toss us overboard, all I could think of was a variation of Sam Goldwyn's remark: "What a hell of a day to spend Sunday!"

I tried to divert myself by pencilling our radio calls on the scarf ring—strike leader, Melrose 188; squadron leader, 201; ourselves, 212—but my pencil broke, and getting out my knife to sharpen it, I laid my thumb open. Pappy Harshman broke into my bitching with "Stand by to start engines!" A crewman slipped the braces from our wings and tail. Billy gunned his engine. Hank Pierson gave me a thumbs-up from the base of the island, and Bob Doyle waved from flag bridge. We took the air at 1443.

I'd brought a camera along, around my neck, so while we were circling I snapped the task group, in the fervent hope that it would be intact when we returned. By the time I'd finished, the flight had joined up: eleven of us 2Cs and eleven TBMs, with four F6s as cover.

Tail-end Charlie always has a lonely time. Number 104, to port, was the only plane near us, and the sun struck his canopy at such an angle that I couldn't see the gunner, to practice hand-taps. The sea was calm, but the air was rougher than usual; our port wing and 104's starboard lunged and parried as if they were broadswords. I was happier when Billy hauled away a bit, and I took a picture of 104 as a farewell.

Now I was completely alone. I turned up the radio: "Hello, Handyman. Hello, Handyman. This is Ruby 22, with Ruby 23 and 24. . . . Hello, Handyman. This is Ruby 22, with Ruby 23 and 24. . . . Hello, Handyman!" No answer.

Somebody else; "My compass is out. Give me your compass heading every five minutes, every *f-i-v-e* minutes. . . ."

1533. Land—the little islands off Okinawa's east coast. When we crossed the main island, at Ishikawa, we had a magnificent panorama of war and peace. To the north, the countryside was neat and green and tranquil. Beneath us, the roads through the bottleneck were jammed with traffic —trucks, command cars, field guns, motorcycles, and even

146

farm wagons drawn by horses—all headed south, where the fighting is. Haze and thick smoke hid that end of Okinawa, but as our formation turned to port, southward, hundreds of ships broke clear. The two nearest the beach were hospital ships.

1549. We're circling idly at 2200 feet. A Privateer, its huge tail sticking up like a haystack, lowers its flaps and wheels to land at captured Yontan. Another circle, and another. I wish that Whisky, or whoever is today's target coordinator, would call us in and put us to work. On the other hand, I haven't heard our strike leader report in yet. Whoa! Here's Whisky now: "Hello, 333 Tiger! If you'll move your point of impact just a little up the hill, you'll have him right on the button."

"This is Tiger 333. Roger! . . . Tiger 333 pushing over now."

"Right on, Tiger 333! Nice eye!"

Our fourth circle . . . Our fifth . . .

1603. Our strike leader calls Whisky at last and gives him the composition of the flight, with the bomb loads. When he comes to us 2Cs, he says, "I also have eleven Victor Bakers, each with two 500-pounders and two 250-pounders, all instantaneous. Our Easy Tare Dog is shackle Mike Charlie Dog Victor."

Whisky: "Roger, 188 Melrose. Thank you. Out."

Our sixth circle. . . .

A cryptic fragment from the phones: "Hello, [garble] Base. This is [garble] 1. Mother says, 'Nan William.' "

1615. Our seventh circle. . . . Suddenly I notice that the red tab on our starboard wing is sticking up, indicating that the wing is not locked, and report it to Billy. It doesn't alarm him at all. "Oh, *that's* nothing," he assures me.

Here's Whisky again: "Hello, Melrose 188. A strike is now going on. Soon as it's out of the way, I'll call you in."

"Roger, Whisky. Out."

Our eighth circle . . . Nuts to this! The old battleships below us are turning to starboard, scalloping the smooth seas. Our ninth . . . We've been horsing around for more than half an hour now. Come on, Whisky, let's do the job and get out of here! "If you're goin' to marry me, marry me, Bill, an' quit this muckin' abaht!"

Whisky obliged: "Hello, 188 Melrose. Your target area is 7066 Easy."

"Roger, Whisky . . . Hello, 201 Melrose. This is 188 Melrose. Did you receive that?"

Our squadron leader answers, "Affirmative."

"Then break off your Victor Bakers and take them over there."

The Air Support chart showed target area 7066 E to be a gun emplacement—one of four—on the eastern tip of Senaga Shima, a small island about 500 yards offshore from Naha. The bombers headed south, and presently I could see Senaga Shima itself. I put my glasses on it. The guns were big ones; I could tell that they were at least 5-inchers, but not if they were dual-purpose. When we were dead over them, at 3500 feet, our squadron leader reported, "On station!"

"Roger," Whisky said. "Don't go down too low! There's a lot of AA there."

"Roger. May we climb for altitude now?"

"Affirmative."

I watched the guns anxiously as we spiraled up. We entered a spotty undercast at 4000 feet, and I lost them, but none had fired by then. Still, Whisky warned us again, "I suggest you precede your attack with fighter strafing. That AA may be *really* bad!"

1710. We're at 6600 feet now, and our phones go crazy all of a sudden, hissing and crackling. The Japs have broken into our radio channel. This is the first time I've heard them since L-Day at Bougainville, when they screamed, for some inscrutable reason, "Hello, Joe! It's beautifur! It's beautifur!", over and over again. Today they're talking Japanese, so I have no idea what they're saying.

1720. We're circling at 7000 feet, waiting for the fighters to finish strafing the target. We're right over it, evidently we're going to dive, not glide. Yes, there goes the first plane!—"dropping," as bomber pilots always declare, "like a —— from a tall cow." I haven't made a dive since the strike on Agana last July, and I'm not sure that my plumbing is still in practice. I'd pull my belt tight if I could get at it under all this harness, but I can only hug my belly and hope. Nine bombers have gone now. One more, then us, the last. Here it comes. . . . Billy yells, "Get set!", cocks his starboard wing, and the camera and binoculars around my neck stand straight out in front of me. The altimeter begins to spin backwards, and I begin to scream, to blunt the air-pressure daggers trying to pierce my eardrums.

At 900 feet, the plane jumps violently. Billy has salvoed his four bombs. I lean from the cockpit to watch them hit, but smoke from earlier bombs boils around us, blinding me. The scream worked. My ears hurt much less than usual.

Billy climbed back to 2000 feet and headed for the rendezvous point. I called him: "Bull's-eye?"

"Couldn't tell."

We overhauled the rest of the strike and took position on 104's wing, jiggling and bouncing in the rough air. My pack of Life Savers fit into the message tube nicely, so I ran it through to Billy and settled back with a cigarette. At 1805, the radio said, "Hello, Melrose Base. This is 188 Melrose. I see you. I see you. Approaching on sector Uncle." The task group was ahead of us. I counted the ships with my fingers crossed: one CV, three CVLs, two BBs, two CBs, one CL, and eight DDs—all present, thank God! Those three GQs before our take-off must have exhausted the quota for the day.

Billy called back, "Chute off and safety belt latched?"

"Affirmative."

He breezed us in to a perfect landing. The ship looked odd as we made our way along the portside catwalk. Suddenly I realized why: it was at GQ—the sixth of the afternoon, somebody said. During one of them, a Myrt had orbited above the task group at 33,000 feet. Our gunners could see it clearly, entirely white, but they couldn't reach it. Our fighters could, though. Diving to get away from them, the Myrt pulled off one of its wings.

Church service had to wait until we secured, at 2015.

April 23rd. At sea

We're fueling tomorrow, and Captain Combs shoves off for Manila. His new job carries a lot of prestige, including a promotion to rear admiral (Proff will be his flag lieutenant), but there's not a man aboard who doesn't hate for him to take it. He and the exec have made the *Yorktown* a happy ship and a proud one. We hope to God that Captain Boone, our new skipper, can keep her so.

The ceremony of changing the command was held on the flight deck this afternoon, between flight operations. Admiral Radford gave Captain Combs the Legion of Merit with a fine citation, and the exec gave him a brand new two-star flag. "You'll notice, sir," he said, "we've left plenty of room on it for your future stars."

Then both captains read their orders, and the ceremony was over.

Big discussion in the wardroom tonight about getting someone to design a "Fighting Lady" emblem, possibly to be
painted on our stack. Walt Disney had done so many combat
emblems that it was natural for us to think in terms of
cartoons. Fontaine Fox's "Powerful Katrinka" was rejected
as too gentle. "Joan L. Sullivan," in the "Li'l Abner" strip,
isn't famous enough. We finally agreed on another of Al
Capp's characters, "Mammy Yokum," and I promised to
write Capp when I got home. (But I didn't; I never thought
of it again.)

Dick Tripp is leaving tomorrow, too, for Uncle Sugar, so
—since we're retiring to fuel, and the possibility of action
is slim—Hank Reis gave him a *despedida* in their room.
Someone brought a pint of torp. The moment it was un-
corked, the smell flooded the room, wafting me back to
Munda. . . .

One of Gus Widhelm's night fighters, "Steep" Hill, had
invited me over to their hut for a cocktail. I didn't watch
him make them. I just took the container he handed me—
a can that had originally held salted peanuts—and when he
said, "Here's kindness!", I clinked and drank. I felt as if
I'd swallowed an overcoat button, with my finger on an
open switch.

"What's the matter?" Steep asked. "Some go down the
wrong way?"

Several minutes passed before I could answer. "No," I
said. "No, I—look: what *is* this stuff?"

"Why, torp. Nothing but torp, with some fixin's."

"What's torp and what are the fixin's?"

It appeared that "torp" is short for "torpedo juice," the
alcohol they sometimes use as fuel. It may be a special,
beefed-up, high-octane kind, but I don't think so and I
never asked. In the Solomons, you didn't investigate the
chemical composition of your drinks any more than you in-
vestigated their source. The "fixin's" were, in this case,
canned grapefruit juice, although canned pineapple juice
was usually preferred. Whichever was served, the drink was
always known as "Condition Red" (meaning "air attack
imminent or in progress").

Tripp and Reis knew the conventions of drinking torp,
but the others didn't, so we briefed them. The most important point is always to use torpedo terminology. For instance,
when the host asks how big a drink you want, you mustn't
say, "A short one, please," but "Oh, about a 400-yard run."

And when, next day, you compare notes on the party, it is *de rigueur* to state either "I ran hot, straight, and true" (got pleasantly tight) or "I broached and porpoised" (got staggering drunk).

The second phrase has far greater currency, because torp's chief effect is confusion, of the senses as well as the limbs. I remember a brilliant moonlit night on New Georgia when a dignified commander started home to his tent, 20 yards away, but returned almost immediately, protesting, "There's a weather front out there that a mouse couldn't get through!"

I also remember that when our command moved up to Bougainville, not even torp was obtainable, and we were reduced to drinking varnish thinner. (At least, that's what the label on the can said.) My tentmates included a Marine major, a dive-bomber pilot, with a talent for puns. One afternoon a Navy Catalina was overdue with some supplies we needed, and the major asked, "Quo usque tandem abutere, Catilina, patientia nostra?" His pun on the varnish thinner wasn't that elaborate, but it was still pretty good. He caught us drinking it and remarked coldly, "All lacquered up, I see."

The best pun I ever heard in the Navy, I can date exactly: June 18, 1944. That was the day of the famous Marianas "turkey-shoot," when Admiral Mitscher's Task Force 58 knocked down more than 400 Jap planes in a few hours. I was on the *Lexington* then, and the lieutenant who shared my battle station was also an alumnus of Munda and Bougainville. When the attack reached its full fury, and Jap planes were flaming all around the horizon, he lifted his flashproof mask long enough to shout in my ear, "The Solomons in all their glory had not a raid like one of these!"

Now what price FPA's "snare Andalusian" and George Kaufman's "I have been trey-deuced"?

April 24th. At sea

The phone rang early this morning, and a broken voice cried, "You bastardo, what have-a you *done* to me?"

"Signor Riccardo Trippini," as Dick calls himself in such times of great stress, was evidently broaching and porpoising.

I saw him and Captain Combs and Proff transfer to the tanker, and watched our mailbags come aboard.

I read each of my letters three times over, as usual, then fell asleep. When I woke up, I found that we'd received two welcome presents: the *Iowa* and the *Shangri La*. The CV makes us happier than the BB does. The *kamikazes'* favorite targets are CVs. The *Yorktown* has been the only one in our task group for the past few days, so the *Shangri La* should split the next attack.

Tonight Les Brown, Doc Lenhardt, Nick Cline and I had a discussion of the supreme physical pleasure. The expectable favorite was scarcely mentioned. All four of us, raw with crud, gave our votes to a good, thorough scratching.

April 25th. At sea

The Admiral tells me my job is finished; I'll be detached on the 28th, when we fuel next, and a CVE will give me a lift to Guam, where I can catch a plane to Pearl. This is as far as his authority runs, he said, but he's pretty sure that COMAIRPAC will send me the rest of the way home. O frabjous day! Callooh! Callay!

April 26th. At sea

Ready 3 has a new piece of bric-a-brac, a Jap skull which Ed Wiezorek brought back from Okinawa as a souvenir of his crash landing last Sunday. It was rather obviously fresh, and was grislier for having belonged to the archetypal Jap of American caricature—the front teeth in its upper jaw stuck straight out.

I'd gone to Ready 3 to accept a farewell present from Bombing 9, a last Okinawa hop. When the ticker rattled off our flight data, and the bomber pilots read that the fighters escorting us would be carrying thousand-pounders (a heavy load for a fighter plane), one of them shouted, "Let's go topside and watch 'em dribble off the bow!" We ourselves are also carrying a thousand-pounder apiece, plus two 250-pound wing bombs. The pilot, Billy May, told me, "We've drawn old 111 today. Know which one I mean?" I certainly did. She's my favorite in the squadron, for no better reason than that she's dark blue all over, whereas the other 2Cs have gray bellies.

I climbed aboard and plugged in the phones. The first words I caught nearly made me climb out again: "—I estimate about seven of the bastards, and another bunch above that." I didn't know who was talking; I hoped it was someone over Germany.

We roared across the ramp at 1153 and circled the task group—a pretty hefty one, now that it's been beefed up by the *Iowa* and the *Shangri La*. My comfortable reflections were interrupted by the radio. As soon as our strike, "Support Dog" again, was clear of the area, the returning strike had begun to land, and the leader of its bombers thought he was in trouble, because he was telling his wingmen, "Hello, Melrose 202 or 203. This is Melrose 201. Come over here and see if my wheels are fully extended."

The *Yorktown* beat them to the report: "This is Melrose Base. Your wheels are OK."

Then a stranger took the air: "This is Pelican 77. I am circling two survivors, one in evergreen, the other in life jacket. I have—"

Our strike leader broke in, "Hello, Sharpshooter. This is Melrose 99. Do you see us?"

"Affirmative."

"Roger, Sharpshooter. Hello, Melrose Base. This is Melrose 99. Departing for target. Out."

"Sharpshooter" is the *Shangri La*, which is sharing this strike with us. Her planes join up gracefully and ride on our port quarter—six TBMs and six SB2Cs, with four F4Us providing portside cover. The *Yorktown* has sent a similar group, except that our fighters, off to starboard, are F6Fs.

The twin formation heads for the target at 750 feet, and even at this low altitude the ceiling is right on top of us. When it bulges downward, our props bite out chunks and whisk them astern. Visibility is less than a mile. If this sour, ugly weather doesn't improve over the target, we'll have a tough time hitting it.

Somebody else is in trouble now: "This is Ruby 43. I just took off and I've got smoke coming out of my cowling. I believe I'd better put her back on the deck." No answer. "Ruby" is another stranger; none of our carriers has this call sign. A third stranger drawls, "Bo-gey is friend-ly. . . ."

1231. Okinawa is in sight, but only just. The clouds, broken but still thick, are squatting on the peaks of the higher mountains. We cross the island farther north than usual. What I can see of it through the holes is much wilder than the southern part. There are no villages here, merely a few small clusters of thatched huts, exactly like those we used to spot in New Guinea and the Solomons, except that the land around them isn't cleared. Southward, the mountains are terraced with fields, and villages begin to appear.

One is burnt out completely; nothing is left but some red tiles scattered among the ashes.

1249. Our strike leader reports to Whisky, and Whisky assigns us to target areas 8170 Mike and Roger. This has a familiar sound, and no wonder: the chart shows it to be that same damned old battery we tried to hit on the 19th! —the one in those hillside caves. The sheltering hill is too steep for a dive bomber to hit the cave mouths, and the facing hill screens them from low-level skip-bombing. This attack will be a bloody waste of bombs and gas and time. Nuts to it!

As we circle for altitude, we get glimpses of both coasts. The number of ships in the bay just above Naha has almost doubled since we were here four days ago; I can count 22 Libertys alone. The east coast is being patrolled by cruisers; every now and then a turret winks, and three spouts of earth shoot up inland.

1316. Billy rocks his wings and pushes over from 7,000 feet. At once the Aldis lamp breaks loose from its clips, and our corkscrew dive rattles it around in our bilges. I scrunched down in my seat to grab it before it shattered, so I didn't see our bomb hit, and presently I didn't care. The pull-out drove my stomach through my shoes. . . .

I was still gulping and swallowing when Billy climbed back to 4,000 feet and pushed over again, to drop our wing bombs. This time I watched them fall, but lost them in the smoke and dust around the target. The second pull-out was worse than the first. . . .

The radio helped me get my mind off the turmoil in my throat. Two fighters were talking: "Sorry, but I couldn't see your rocket."

"I saw it. It just plummeted along the ground, not proving a goddam thing."

Another voice: "—Just south of the sugar factory. Tell the last man in your formation to be careful!"

The phones went quiet then, and I was left with myself for company for the whole ride home. When we landed, I tottered down to my sack and crawled in.

A shower and a hot supper worked such wonders, though, that Hendy and I challenged Bill Dietrich and Barney Kegan to a final bridge match at double stakes. The cards loved us; we held one barnburner after another and were 2800 points in front when Air Defense blew. The bogey's behavior was odd: it closed slowly, but climbed extremely fast. When it reached the unprecedented height of 44,000 feet, CIC figured it had to be an escaped barrage balloon, and passed the word to secure. I must have brought flag bridge's chill to my bridge in the wardroom, because Hendy and I never won another rubber.

April 27th. At sea

A quiet day, with no GQs and not even an Air Defense, so I was able to pack my gear for tomorrow, say my good-byes, and collect messages for delivery at home. One of my first calls—at Pat Patterson's room—threw the rest of my schedule out of joint, because we began to talk dogs and birds and guns, and the steel bulkheads melted into briar patches and fields of broomstraw, and the hours ran past us unheeded. Only once did we let war intrude, and even then it was another war. Pat had been telling me about stalking wild turkeys with a high-power .22 and a 'scope, and he broke off to ask, "Did you know I'd been a sniper in the first World War?"

I settled back and listened.

"Yessuh, long befo' America came in, I went up to Canada and 'listed. The recruitin' officer ast me, 'What part Canada you f'um, son?' Well, suh, the only place in all Canada I could lay my tongue to was Prince Rupert Island, 'cause my uncle had been there oncet on a huntin' trip. I didn't know where it was or anything 'bout it, but I took a gamble, and six weeks later I was in France, snipin'. I used to hide out in the bushes with a li'l ole piece of cheese an' a li'l ole hunk of bread an' a li'l ole bottle of wine, an' one day I saw this German colonel an' other officers right out in the open, comin' right straight at me. I took a sight on the colonel's th'oat, an' when they got close 'nough, I tol' 'em, 'Surrender!', an' took 'em in. Li'l while, the colonel sent for me an' called me a goddam fool.

"I ast, 'Why's that, suh?'

"He said, ' 'Cause when*ever* you see a colonel, shoot him!' "

I also fell to talking with Bob Brandt. "It's a funny outfit, this Navy," he said. "Ever since I've been in it, I've hit all the right places at the wrong times: Georgia in the summer, Atlantic City in the winter, and the Pacific when there was a war on."

Last good-byes and last collection of messages. The Admiral's was, "Tell those people at COMAIRPAC they can't leave us here forever! That's the way they lost their carriers at Guadalcanal—keeping them in the same place too long."

1015. I took my gear down to the fantail. My taxi destroyer, the *Hazelwood,* came under our counter; lines were passed, and I was stepping into the canvas sack when Commander Brady said, "Souvenir of the cruise," and handed me a silver bos'n's pipe, bless him!

I thought I was going to get a ducking on the way across, but it was a dry trip. The *Hazelwood's* officers invited me to the wardroom for coffee. When they learned I was from the staff, they wanted me to identify the staff voices on the TBS.

"Who's the one that talks in that clipped way, the one who says, 'Ex-cute!' "

"That's Jimmy Smith, assistant Operations for Air."

"He's plenty good, that boy. Who's the one who said, 'I hear you two by two—too loud and too often'?"

I didn't know. I guess only the Admiral would dare say it, but I've never seen him get mad enough.

"Well, who's the guy that puts *uh* on the end of everything? 'Hello, Curio-*uh,* this is Melrose-*uh.*' And what the hell's the point? Does he think he's making himself any clearer, or is he just bilious?"

I didn't have to answer. Just then the *Hazelwood* stood in toward an escort carrier, the *Windham Bay,* and we all went out on the fo'c'sle to see her. Twice as many men were standing by as would possibly be needed to handle the lines. I wondered why, until somebody explained that they were eager to learn what films the *Windham Bay* was bringing them.

As we stood away, one of the *Hazelwood's* officers took me up to the bridge and introduced me to their skipper, Comdr. Volckert P. Douw, a crisp, smart-looking man, with the warmest smile I've ever seen. We chatted a few minutes, then he said, "I bet you don't know who you're talking to. No? I'll tell you: you're talking to the happiest guy in the whole goddam Navy! See that man standing there?"—he pointed to the other wing of the bridge—"That's my relief. He's going to take over in a couple of days, and I'll go home and see my wife and kids for the first time in God knows when."

We were coming alongside another CVE, the *Attu*, which was giving me a lift to Guam, so I told the skipper good-bye and wished him well. He had no messages for me to send his wife; he thought he'd get home before I would.

A piece of luck! The *Attu's* exec is my old friend Hays Browning. He gave me a big, comfortable room, and two minutes later I was asleep. I slept all afternoon, staggered down to the wardroom for supper, and slept 14 hours that night.

April 29th (Sunday). At sea

The talk at breakfast was about the attack on the *Comfort* at Okinawa last night. Despite her unmistakable markings as a hospital ship—white paint, large green crosses, and floodlighting—a *kamikaze* crashed into her, inflicting casualties that included a number of patients with battle wounds. The wardroom's opinion was about evenly divided between outrage at the inhumanity of the attack and contempt for its stupidity. The latter point of view seems callous, but it's militarily sound; caring for its wounded is a far greater drain on a nation at war than burying its dead.

Church service, on the hangar deck, brought another variation of the Navy hymn, "Eternal Father, Strong to Save." The new stanza runs,

> *When storms are nigh and clouds are dark,*
> *Guide Thou the hand that steers their bark.*
> *Far above the land and sea*
> *By day and night their Pilot be.*
> *Hear, oh, hear our earnest prayer*
> *For all who travel through the air.*

"Steers their bark" offends me; it's artificial, poetastric. I'd prefer,

> *Through fog and night and storm and rain*
> *Guide Thou the hand that guides their plane.*

After church, a bos'n's mate gave me a lesson on my new pipe. It needs tuning, he said. First I knew that they *could* be tuned. The Chief Engineer, Leif Erickson, told me that bos'ns in the old Navy—"the kind who didn't put on a pair of shoes for 25 years"—had pipes that cost up to $150, solid silver ones, inlaid with gold.

Slept through the afternoon.

April 30th. At sea

My birthday. I'll never forget the last one, when midnight of the 29th found me in a Marine R4C, 12,000 feet above the Pacific. I couldn't sleep, because I was too damned cold. I couldn't talk with anyone, because I was the only passenger. I couldn't read, because the plane was blacked out. And I couldn't smoke, because the cargo space was packed with tanks of extra fuel. My God, what an interminable night!

This morning Hays took me up to the bridge and gave me the long glass and pointed to a destroyer on our starboard beam. "Look at that mess," he said.

Her bridge was mashed flat. Her foremast was hanging over the side. The starboard 40mm mount was lying on the deck.

Hays said, "A *kamikaze* hit her Saturday afternoon, just after you came aboard. I saw the dispatch, but I've forgotten the exact number of casualties. I know she's requesting a new skipper."

I put the glass on her bow. Her number stood out clearly: "531"—the *Hazelwood.*

The happiest guy in the whole goddam Navy
A million laughs, chum—a million of'em!
I'll never forget *this* birthday, either.

EPILOGUE

May. Washington

Jimmy Smith was detached from the *Yorktown* a few days after me. He overtook me at Pearl, and we came home together. Soon after we'd reported to the Navy Department, he stopped by to say that he'd run into an acquaintance of his, a captain, in the Bureau of Aeronautics.

The captain asked, "How was it out there?"

"Pretty rugged," Jimmy said. "Those *kamikazes*—"

The captain interrupted, "Lemme tell you something that happened *here* the other day. I had to get this Army colonel out to a picnic, so I called up the Army and asked if they'd furnish us a jeep. Do you think those bastards would lend me one? Like hell they would! Rugged? You don't know what rugged is!"

BALLANTINE WAR BOOKS

Ballantine War Books are a new series designed to bring the whole story of dramatic, important events in World War II to the buyer of low-priced books. Here, often for the first time, is told the inside story of decisive campaigns and important command decisions. In these books enemy leaders tell of their achievements and their problems. These are the stories that couldn't be told until long after the war ended. Now, with enemy records at last available these Ballantine War Books present the whole and complete picture of enemy and Allied actions. New titles are added each month; watch for them to appear in this series:

        "The memoirs of Hitler's foremost tank expert contain some of the most interesting writing there has been—from that side—about the last war."—*The New Yorker*

(When ordering by mail, quantities of less than four books, please include 5¢ postage for each tile.)

Ballantine Books, Inc., 101 Fifth Avenue, New York 3, N. Y.